SP 21

PR
4757
.E5
G7
1962

Grimsditch, Herbert Borthwick, 1898–
Character and environment in the novels of Thomas
Hardy. New York, Russell & Russell, 1962.

188 p. 23 cm.

Includes bibliography

1. Hardy, Thomas, 1840–1928.

PR4757.E5G7 1962   823.8   62—13835 ‡

Library of Congress   [66f2]

CHARACTER & ENVIRONMENT
IN THE NOVELS OF
THOMAS HARDY

CHARACTER AND ENVIRONMENT IN THE NOVELS OF THOMAS HARDY

By Herbert B. Grimsditch, M.A.

NEW YORK

RUSSELL & RUSSELL · INC

1962

FIRST PUBLISHED IN 1925
REISSUED, 1962, BY RUSSELL & RUSSELL, INC.
BY ARRANGEMENT WITH H. F. & G. WITHERBY LTD. LONDON
L. C. CATALOG CARD NO: 62—13835

PRINTED IN THE UNITED STATES OF AMERICA

PR
1757
.E5
G7
1962

TO
MY PARENTS

" 'Tis all a Chequer-board of Nights and Days
Where Destiny with Men for Pieces plays :
*   Hither and thither moves, and mates, and slays,*
And one by one back in the Closet lays."

FOREWORD

THIS book, as its title and length suggest, is not a comprehensive study of Mr Hardy's works, but is intended rather as an attempt to supplement the various excellent general estimates already published. The Introduction sets forth its purpose, which is, in brief, the examination of a particular aspect of the Wessex Novels in a more detailed fashion than would be possible in a full-length criticism. The principal characters are studied with special reference to their development under the influence of environment, (taking that word in its widest significance), and each is considered in its relationship to the metaphysical hypotheses which are the salient characteristics of Mr Hardy's thought. Since human nature and works of art are not susceptible to the rigid classification which can be employed in science, it need hardly be said that the chapter headings merely represent an effort to attain to that orderly arrangement which is the first condition of any logical appraisal.

It is a pleasure to acknowledge a general debt to those writers whose names appear in the List of Works Consulted; and wherever special acknowledgment is due it has been made, either in the text or in a footnote. In the interests of easy reading, footnotes

FOREWORD

have been given only where they seemed indispensable. All page references to the novels are to Messrs Macmillan's " Wessex Edition."

Throughout the text the prefix " Mr " has been omitted in allusions to the eminent author under criticism. His high place in literature is secure while he is yet happily with us, and it seemed more fitting to speak of him as we speak of Fielding, or Keats, or Dickens ; for with such great names as these will his be handed down.

H. B. G.

CONTENTS

INTRODUCTION

THE novelist, as distinguished from the romance-writer, must grapple with the problems of human character and conduct ; and though he approaches these problems as an observer rather than a moralist it is almost inevitable that he should betray a leaning towards certain types, and thus indirectly champion his own ethical views. But, while he can hardly avoid ethical valuations, he need not necessarily connect the particular with the general and envisage mankind's place and function in the cosmic scheme. This invasion of the realm of metaphysics is the most outstanding characteristic of Thomas Hardy's art, whether in prose or verse. A *positive* metaphysician he is not. He is curiously anxious to point out, on every available occasion, that he lays down no definite system to account for the constitution of the universe ; and he takes exception to statements about his " views," which he would rather term " explorations of reality." One of his latest prefaces, the " Apology " to *Late Lyrics and Earlier* (1922), reiterates in no uncertain terms this protest which he has often made against being saddled with definite convictions relative to the ultimate reality underlying the scheme of things ; so that when

11

" views " or " opinions " are here mentioned it should be understood that these words are employed merely for the sake of convenience.

After his first essay in fiction, *Desperate Remedies,* which is immature and melodramatic, the philosophic attitude which has come to be associated with Hardy's name became more and more clearly defined. His second book, *Under the Greenwood Tree,* contains no more than a few hints of it, but from that time forward it became more and more pronounced, and reached its fullest expression in *The Dynasts.* It strongly colours the fabric of the greater novels, and it would be as impossible to understand Hardy without examining it very fully as to understand Dickens or Jane Austen without taking into account the humour of the one or the irony of the other.

Nevertheless, Hardy's primary purpose is the artistic expression of ideas drawn from his experience of life, not the didactic inculcation of principles. The second of these intentions may produce a *Nature and Art,* but it will not bring forth a novel of high artistic value, for it leads its practitioner into exaggeration and perversion of fact in the effort to bear out a preconceived theory. Hardy follows the better method of looking at the world first and then formulating his conclusions from what he finds there. The word " realism " is often used to signify a method which accumulates unnecessary and tiresome detail, and dwells overmuch on the sordid and revolting aspects of life, but, like many another good

12

INTRODUCTION

word, it has been degraded by a too close association with a particular school or dogma. The views of those who plead for a wider application of the term are well summed up by M. Gustave Reynier in his book, *Les Origines du Roman réaliste*, published in 1912. Realistic art, he says :

" essaie de se tenir aussi près que possible de la vie et d'en rendre à la fois la complexité et la logique, non par une accumulation de détails inertes, mais en choisissant les traits qui caractérisent les individus et les circonstances qui expliquent les faits. Il s'oppose également à ce qui simplifie à l'excès, à ce qui exagère, à ce qui embellit ou enlaidit le modèle, aux conventions des contes à rire comme à celles des fictions idéalistes."

It is in this sense only that Hardy's art is " realistic." Once we have put aside the specialised and con-demnatory usage of the word " realist," it will be seen that this word is the best we can use to describe not only Hardy, but any great novelist. To say this is not, of course, to say that an author is precluded from using, for example, the supernatural, because nowadays most educated people unhesitatingly reject it as an explanation of the unusual. There will always be room for profitable exercise of the im-agination on such masterpieces as *The Haunters and the Haunted*, read with a Coleridgean "suspension of disbelief," and Hardy himself has one story (*The Withered Arm*) in which there is small hint of any explanation by rational means. But the tendency of

modern times is to regard the novel, properly so
called, mainly as a transcript from the book of human
experience, idealised and given shape and coherence
by the artist's composition and exclusion of unnecessary detail ; to demand not only sound psychology,
but also that the interplay of character shall produce
situations such as we can credibly imagine arising in
the actual world as we know it. Mere imitation, without concentration, selection and the " transforming
touch " would produce a result differing as much
from true art as does a newspaper report of a
trial from the stories of Sir Arthur Conan Doyle
or Mr J. S. Fletcher. Leaving aside, however, this
perversion of the Aristotelean doctrine, we find that
a realistic novelist's status (in the wider sense) largely
depends on his attainment of a technical method
whereby he can move our emotions without doing
violence to our reason. From the purely literary
standpoint, then, the question to be answered is not
whether Hardy's metaphysical " opinions " are ob-
jectively true. We have to inquire rather : Is his
reading of character sound ? Is his management of
plot and situation sure ? Are the conclusions he
draws as to life and destiny the natural reaction of
a certain temperament to experience working on it ?
And does his work as a whole create that pleasurable
sympathy of mind and heart which is the indispensable
effect of all great art whatsoever ?

To arrive at a true estimate, it is necessary
to examine the novels in the light of their author's

14

distinctive philosophy. As early as his twenty-seventh year he expressed, in elementary form, his conception of the power of blind chance over percipient man, in the poem *Hap* (1866, not published till 1898). *A Pair of Blue Eyes* (1873), his third novel, is interesting, apart from its intrinsic merits, as the first clear and elaborated embodiment of those views which have come to be associated with Hardy's name. In spite of William Worm (not the least amusing of the long gallery of peasant portraits) it is poorer than its predecessor, *Under the Greenwood Tree*, in humour and its display of that intimate knowledge of country scenes and people which its creator possesses more markedly than any other English novelist; but it exhibits a set of characters in the web of a relentless fate, which seems to enforce its decrees with bitter irony. It brings out the frequency of coincidence and the significance of apparently trifling events. In Knight it gives a first sketch of the hard-hearted, cold, ultra-logical type to which the larger figures of Clare and Yeobright belong, and in Elfride it presents the first full-length picture of the typical Hardy woman. Elfride is one of the most closely studied of the Wessex " heroines," and in many ways the most charming ; but she is impulsive to a fault, vacillating, deceitful and a moral coward, and yet contrives to excite a great deal of affection and sympathy in spite of these drawbacks.

Indeed a certain amount of sympathy is produced in the reader's mind by very nearly all the characters of Hardy, and this has an important bearing on his general outlook. Why do we feel it ? We have no qualms about condemning Sikes or Glossin, because we feel that they are unmitigated scoundrels. But Hardy has no unmitigated scoundrels, because he has reached a conclusion, which is gradually being borne in on the minds of men, that, outside the ranks of the moral perverts (who are mentally abnormal), there is no such thing as a *complete* rogue. Deep-rooted in his mind is a vast, all-embracing love, taking in not only humanity but also the lower animals, and even trees and flowers, though he nowhere seems to attribute consciousness to vegetable nature as Wordsworth does : the sighing of the pines because " they are sorry to begin life in earnest "[1] is a fancy of Marty's, not Hardy's, and is very beautifully in keeping and symbolical of Marty's philosophy, learned in a hard school. When he comes to persons, we have not heroes and villains but simply fallible human beings, none of whom is wholly bad. Examining the characters which most nearly approach a state of unrelieved iniquity, we find that they are five in number, and that these five are the figures in the Wessex Novels which approximate the most closely to conventional types. Manston and Dare are vicious illegitimate sons, of the line of Edmund in *Lear* ; Troy is the soldier heart-breaker of ballad and romance ; Derriman is a very ridiculous *miles gloriosus* ; D'Urberville is in all essentials the

[1] *The Woodlanders*, p. 73.

16

typical conventional seducer, wealthy, impudent and possessed of "a well-groomed black moustache with curled points" and a "bold rolling eye." In other words, it is only when Hardy lapses into conventionality that he produces "villains" pure and simple.

A second consideration arising out of this lack of absolute goodness or badness in the various men and women is that those persons are happiest, but not necessarily *best, who are most in harmony with their environment.* Here we come close to the central point of Hardy's tentative metaphysic. Surveying man in the light of his strong and sympathetic cast of mind, seeing him, not "born in sin," but a being of immense aspirations towards good, he has sought a reason why those aspirations so often come to naught : and the answer to his questioning is that man is the creature of circumstance, a pawn in the game played by destiny. Destiny subjects him to a number of external influences, the sum-total of which makes up his environment, and this plays a large part in the development of his character. Furthermore, that residuum, that internal composition, which is never the same in any two men, helps to determine a person's reaction to such influences for good or evil. It may be so tainted that it vitiates the whole life of its possessor, in which event "character is fate" (as he quotes from Novalis in *The Mayor of Casterbridge*), and the man works his own destruction. Henchard and Jude are the two most striking

17

examples of this. It has already been remarked that
Hardy is at pains to make it clear that no dogmatic
metaphysical doctrine is to be inferred from anything
he writes, and that the " view " of existence underlying his works is (as he puts it in the Preface to
Jude) to be regarded as " a series of seemings or personal impressions, the question of their consistency
or their discordance, their permanence or their
transitoriness, being regarded as not of the first
moment." Bearing this in mind, it is yet desirable,
and indeed necessary (if we are to understand him),
to extract certain definite principles which form, as
it were, his working hypotheses.

Hardy has always been that higher kind of artist
who is a thinker too, and, as such, it would not be surprising to find him seized with the philosophic passion
—the desire to frame some coherent, unifying conception of the universe. It is clear that the seeming
incoherence and inconsistency of things are irksome
to him, but it is equally clear that such answers as
he has evolved to his questionings have not formed
themselves into a cut-and-dried system, and that
they remain " a series of fugitive impressions " [1] to
the last. Writing in an age of great scientific and
philosophic activity, he could hardly fail to be influenced by the spirit of his time. To mention only
one of the great forces, Darwin had revolutionised
the general idea of life so that, after him, human
thought could no longer run in the same channels.

---

[1] Preface, *Late Lyrics and Earlier*. 1922.

INTRODUCTION

Of him Haeckel says that : " As Copernicus (1543) gave the death-blow to the geocentric dogma, so did Darwin (1859) to the anthropocentric one closely associated with it." [1] The striking passages in *Two on a Tower* on the immensity and awfulness of space reveal a mind which has far outgrown any exaggerated idea of the earth's importance ; and likewise the argument that Tess has broken no natural law evinces a mental attitude which looks upon man not as an absolutely unique phenomenon, but rather as the elder brother in a family. This point of view arises naturally out of the acceptance of the theory of evolution, and it has ramifications too wide to be followed here.

Side by side with the question of the physical nature and origin of man, and intimately bound up with it, are such ancient philosophical problems as those of evil and the freedom of the will. These Hardy may be said to have approached from two sides—the philosophic and (for want of a better word) the " human." His logical reasoning shows him that it is impossible to reconcile the benevolence of an omnipotent and omniscient deity with the fact of evil.[2] The freedom of the will, looked at in the light of the same reasoning, cannot be other than an illusion,[3] for a break in the chain of cause and

[1] *Monism*, trs. Gilchrist. 1903.

[2] Vide *A Dream Question* (*Time's Laughing-Stocks*).

[3] The nearest approach to an admission of freedom of the will is in the Apology to *Late Lyrics and Earlier*, where he speaks of " the modicum of free will conjecturally possessed by

19

effect (such as "freedom" necessarily connotes) is unthinkable. Man, despite the elevation to which he has risen, is still an animal, as may be readily observed when his passions are aroused. From the philosophic side, then, Hardy's central hypothesis becomes that of an Immanent Will, working through all things by immutable laws, but working like a machine, unconscious of its own operations. This conception may owe something to Schopenhauer, who, in *The World as Will and Idea*, develops at length the thought of Will as the ultimate force. He follows Kant in averring that the world revealed through the sense-perceptions is only phenomenal, and on this side Hardy, as a novelist, has nothing to say. But both are determinists, both look upon Will as the motive-power behind the universe, both describe this Will as blind, and both are pessimists.[1] Schopenhauer's way of escape, however, is through art and benevolence, while Hardy seems to imply that the

organic life when the mighty necessitating forces—unconscious or other—that have 'the balancings of the clouds,' happen to be in equilibrium, which may or may not be often." This, with its "modicum," "conjecturally," "happen" and "may," is very grudging, and is hedged round with doubts.

[1] Hardy, it is true, disowns the term. He quotes his poem, *In Tenebris*:

"If a way to the Better there be, it exacts a full look at the Worst,"

and describes his method as "the exploration of reality, and its frank recognition stage by stage along the survey, with an eye to the best consummation possible: briefly, evolutionary meliorism."—Preface, *Late Lyrics and Earlier*. 1922.

ills of life are best borne by the aid of a brave, stoical resignation. Thus the ethical consequences of his beliefs (whatever may be thought as to the beliefs themselves) result in the upholding of ideals of conduct which have always been approved by the wisest of mankind.

This tentative metaphysic is worked out most fully in *The Dynasts*. The shorter poems (which stand in a similar relation to the epic-drama to that borne by Wordsworth's " cells and oratories " to his " Gothic Church ") express many aspects of it in concentrated form. *Hap* [1] and *The Sign-Seeker* [1] show Fate, not as a malignant power (" that could be endured "), but as a blind and indifferent impulse. In *God-forgotten* [2] the speaker fancies he hears the deity speaking of Earth as one of the worlds he has made long ago and since forgotten. *The Subalterns* [2] are life's evils, crying out to man that they do not wish to injure him, but they too are passive agents; and *A Plaint to Man* [3] and *God's Funeral* [3] present God as a " man-projected Figure." The general tone of these utterances is one of haunting sadness, but sometimes it becomes ironical, as in *The Respectable Burgher and the " Higher Criticism."* [2] The foundering of the *Titanic* forms the text of a powerful poem,[4] which describes the opulent ship

[1] *Wessex Poems.*
[2] *Poems of Past and Present.*
[3] *Time's Laughing-Stocks.*
[4] *The Convergence of the Twain (Satires of Circumstance).*

21

growing up, and, far away in the Arctic solitude, its "sinister mate," the iceberg, likewise forming :

> " Till the Spinner of the Years
>   Said ' Now! ' And each one hears,
> And consummation comes, and jars two hemi-
> spheres."

In this scheme, Nature is a *Sleep-Worker* [1] : she grieves (in *The Mother Mourns* [1]) that man has begun to doubt her perfection ; for she has unwittingly produced a creature capable of reading her defects. Even amidst unconscious life there is conflict.[2] Little hope is held out of any future amelioration of this " sorry scheme of things." There are bare hints of such in *God-forgotten* and *The Darkling Thrush*,[1] and *The Dynasts* closes on a note of hopefulness, though it is given to the " impressionable and inconsistent" [3] Spirit of the Pities. A paragraph in the Preface to *The Dynasts* administers several cautions and admonitions to the reader, in the careful way Hardy often uses in order to avoid misunderstanding. The Spirits are " contrivances of the fancy merely." The remainder of the paragraph is best quoted at length, for it speaks for itself with no uncertain voice :

" The wide acceptance of the Monistic theory of the Universe forbade, in this twentieth century, the

---

[1] *Poems of Past and Present.*

[2] *The Ivy-Wife* and *In a Wood* (*Wessex Poems*).

[3] Preface to *The Dynasts.*

22

importation of Divine personages from any antique Mythology as ready-made sources or channels of Causation, even in verse, and excluded the celestial machinery of, say, *Paradise Lost*, as peremptorily as that of the *Iliad* or the *Eddas*. And the abandonment of the masculine pronoun in allusions to the First or Fundamental Energy seemed a necessary and logical consequence of the long abandonment by thinkers of the anthropomorphic conception of the same."

These are the words of a man who possesses the rare capability of seeing life from the scientific side and at the same time realising all its artistic potentialities. Very seldom are the scientific and poetic visions combined in one mind, and it is indeed from the strife between these viewpoints that Hardy creates his art. It has been said that he approaches the problem of existence not only from the philosophic but also from the human side. It is probably this that prevents his acceptance of Spinoza's idea of one ultimate Substance, of which good and evil are but modes, and might be likened to the plus and minus signs in algebra or the obverse and reverse of one shield. Hardy is too closely in sympathy with the ordinary, simple man to look at the matter in this detached way. He recognises very clearly that the gulf between good and evil is and must remain a painful reality to mankind. Both are due to the workings of the Will, but man has somehow become percipient, feeling the love of good and the hatred of evil, while remaining a pawn in the game : hence

23

INTRODUCTION

" the intolerable antilogy of making figments feel." [1]
Here the philosopher becomes at variance with the
simple man, who feels within him, as all men feel,
that the individual *can* will many of his deeds, that
he *can* choose between good and evil, true and false.
And out of this clash between a determinism arrived
at by logical processes and freedom felt as a deeply
rooted innate belief arises Hardy's tragic apprehension of the world. The irony of the situation is that
man's every action is performed under the urge of
this belief in his freedom, which is nothing but an
illusion.

It needs no deep delving to discover that Hardy
is essentially an ironist and a tragedian. Many of the
novels have a strong affinity with drama. Comedy
there is in abundance ; comedy of a rare, whimsical
strain, like that provided by Poorgrass and the old
maltster (in *Far from the Madding Crowd*) ; or of a
broad, farcical nature, like the stories of Tony Kytes
and of the inebriated choir who played a jig instead
of a hymn (*A Few Crusted Characters*). It is found
even in *Tess of the D'Urbervilles*, the most pathetic
of all the books, and only in *Jude* and some of the
short stories is it altogether lacking. But only in
Under the Greenwood Tree and *A Few Crusted
Characters* (and perhaps *The Hand of Ethelberta*) is
it the predominant note. The note of laughter,
however, sets off and heightens while it relieves the
note of tears. It is generally struck by the simple

[1] *The Dynasts*, p. 100.

24

peasant characters (significantly enough, by those who know least about life) and is sincere and kindly; for though the mirth frequently arises from the author's gently ironical comments, interspersed with the rustic conversation, the irony is never bitter or cynical.

A Pair of Blue Eyes has already been named as the first of the tragedies built up on the deterministic foundation. It also exhibits two other distinctive characteristics of its author in a manner so decided that they have been cited as signs of the immaturity of this book. These are his reliance on coincidence and his fondness for inaugurating great affairs by small and apparently unimportant events. The first point might be exemplified from any of the novels, and has been put down as an artistic defect.[1] Too great a dependence on the " long arm " is undoubtedly a failing, but at the same time it should be remembered that, under a strict deterministic philosophy, there is no such thing as the fortuitous—and every concatenation of events is a coincidence, and is only so called *when we recognise it as such*. Nevertheless this is no sufficient excuse for a too-frequent employment of the coincidence as a means of furthering the action in a novel. Small events do indeed play a great part in setting great events in motion in the Wessex Novels, but they do so also in real life. It is true that the Parson's discovery of the D'Urberville ancestry

---

[1] S. C. Chew (*Thomas Hardy*, 1921, pp. 36-37) notes two pages full of coincidences from *A Pair of Blue Eyes*.

25

and the accident to the horse, Prince, are the immediate and proximate causes of all Tess's misfortunes, but it is also true that a murder at Sarajevo was the match which set all Europe ablaze, and that a criminal has been brought to book by so small a thing as his misspelling of a word in a telegram.

The main materials out of which Hardy constructs his tragedy are the interplay of human emotions and the conflict between the aspirations of conscious man and the absolute law of unconscious fate. Under a system of this nature, the part assigned to environment in the shaping of character is necessarily large. Hardy limits the sphere of action, as a rule, to a certain locality, and draws his personages in the main from one stratum of society. He gains in concentration by this method and shows that it is not necessary to seek out the unusual in order to produce tragedy. The powerful passions which dominate mankind may be watched in operation equally well in Paris or in a place like Little Hintock, "where, from time to time, dramas of a grandeur and unity truly Sophoclean are enacted in the real, by virtue of the concentrated passions and closely-knit interdependence of the lives therein." [1] These passions are found in varying strengths in all men. But the ways in which they manifest themselves are of infinite variety, and are differentiated to a large extent by external conditions. That the plots of the novels mainly turn on love complications

[1] *The Woodlanders*, pp. 4-5.

by no means argues paucity of invention. Hardy perceives that love is " the strongest passion known to humanity " [1] ; that it is quite the deepest, most subtle and most widespread influence in life, and is common to all ranks and classes whatsoever. More than this, it is the only force productive of drama which affects the lives of most people, for such experiences as crime and hazardous adventure come the way of very few.

Hardy obviously writes with the fully conscious purpose of developing his characters consistently in accord with their innate basis (which might be called their *internal* environment), and, secondly, along lines into which they are put by such influences as early training, social rank, custom, convention and the outer world of animate and inanimate nature. Thus he is scientific in the sense in which all great artists have been scientific (though few so consciously as he)—that is to say, his world is the artist's world, with its reflections of all the fancy and beauty of life and its poetic glamour and joy, while its bedrock is accurate and enlightened observation. He says, in effect : " This man does not act in a certain way by accident. His personality has been moulded, for better or for worse, by agencies far more potent than the individual will." Occasionally he becomes explicit, as when he shows that events which Henchard ascribes to " the scheme of some sinister intelligence "—an intelligence, that is, antagonistic

1 Preface to *Jude the Obscure.*

27

in quality—are quite natural sequences of cause and effect, and merely show *indifference* on the part of fate, in spite of the ironical fashion in which they seem to occur.

In an article on *The Profitable Reading of Fiction* (in *The Forum*, March 1888), Hardy writes of the "inevitableness of character and environment in working out destiny" : and the influence of environment is again strongly stressed by one of his classifications of the novels (in the Wessex Edition) —"Novels of Character and Environment." The stories in which it appears most clearly, in the narrower physical sense of "surroundings," are *The Return of the Native* and *An Imaginative Woman (Life's Little Ironies)*, which latter, indeed, carries it as the main motive, and is constructed round a subtle psycho-physical manifestation.

The aim of this study is to consider the principal characters of the novels with special reference to the way in which they are moulded by environment (taking the word in its widest sense), so producing that clash between the individual and an immutable destiny which has been shown as the chief source of Hardy's tragedy. Each character will be grouped under that influence which appears to have been strongest in its development, though many must obviously receive incidental reference in more than one section. In every case, the reaction of the individual will depend, to a large extent, on his or her inward bias.

CHAPTER I

UPBRINGING

THE first quarter of the twentieth century has seen a number of notable works of fiction which trace the progress of their principal characters from birth, or very early years, to maturity, or even give a complete life-history. Such are Mr Compton Mackenzie's *Carnival*, Mr Hugh Walpole's *Fortitude*, Mr J. D. Beresford's *Jacob Stahl* trilogy, and, best of all, Mr Arnold Bennett's *The Old Wives' Tale*, written, as he states in his preface, under the stimulation of Maupassant's *Une Vie*. But this is a recent fashion, and before 1900 the majority of English novels have as their chief characters men and women in the prime of life, because it is in the period between childhood and middle age that those passions and interests with which the novelist is most concerned commonly attain their highest point of development. Such conspicuous exceptions as David Copperfield and Tristram Shandy (who, indeed, actually only succeeds in being born at the end of the book), at once come to mind, but they do not take away from the broad truth of the generalisation. Hardy nowhere presents a full life-history, his

29

nearest approach being in *Jude the Obscure*, where Jude is introduced at the age of eleven years; but in many other instances there are retrospective references to the early, formative years of life, when the mind stores up rich hoards of impressions and registers experience the more telling because it is not, at the time, self-conscious. The natures and attitude of the parents, the size of the family and general home conditions must inevitably react on the child. Though Jude is the only personage of note in the Wessex Novels who is actually introduced in early childhood, the youthful years are not dealt with at length, and it is in *Tess of the D'Urbervilles* that Hardy shows himself most concerned with these factors.

It is hinted that Tess's troubles perhaps began long before she was born, in the lawless lives of her aristocratic ancestors, whose blood sometimes runs all too warmly in her veins. At the same time, it is possible to make too much of Hardy's belief in heredity [1] : it is easy to misconstrue the dramatist by fathering on him the opinions of one of his actors, more especially when the speaker is represented in an unfavourable light. Angel Clare, it is true, gives utterance to stinging words about " decrepit families " in the first bitter moments of his disillusionment, but, considering the man and the occasion, the utmost caution should be used in

[1] Lionel Johnson seems to do this (*The Art of Thomas Hardy*, pp. 262-263).

appraising them. Whatever may be thought on the subject of the hereditary taint, there can be no shadow of doubt that Tess's youth is passed under highly unfavourable conditions. The oft-quoted paragraph about the " passengers in the Durbeyfield ship " calls to mind Samuel Butler's World of the Unborn, in *Erewhon*, and, in a lesser degree, Hardy's own poem, *The Unborn (Time's Laughing-Stocks)*. Butler's wise shades counsel those who wish to be born : " Consider the infinite risk ; to be born of wicked parents and trained in vice ! " —and so on. Hardy's shades, in the poem, inquire hopefully of the earth, and are hurried forth by the Will despite the sad tidings they read in the earth-man's face.

Tess is born of shiftless parents, and not trained at all. John Durbeyfield is utterly weak and foolish, without industry, self-control or common-sense. He can work on occasion, but the mood is not always with him when needed ; his favourite diversion is to fuddle at the inn, and when he learns his illustrious ancestry his behaviour is so absurd as to place him very near the borders of sheer feeble-mindedness. He is not definitely depraved, but totally deficient in strength. His wife, Joan, however, while she has certain solid virtues as a house-wife, displays weakness not only in resolution and intelligence, but also in principle. Her method of " bringing home " her husband from Rolliver's is of a piece with her wild hopes of advancement

31

from the sham D'Urbervilles and her attitude towards Tess's misfortune. In the first instance the temptation of the clandestine drinking-party is too much for her. In the second, her weakness lies in the lack of worldly wisdom, strangely enough ; for in the last she displays that quality in its worst form, showing a lamentable deficiency in moral fibre, or something worse. When Tess comes home from Trantridge, it is not the loss of her child's innocence and happiness that Joan deplores: rather is it Tess's unwillingness and inability to raise the family fortunes by a marriage with D'Urberville. On the second disastrous homecoming, arising as a direct consequence of that which caused the first, Joan can find no comfort for Tess, and reproaches her with foolishness for her confession to Clare. What is the use of her marrying a gentleman and then throwing away her advantage in this manner ? To her, Tess is a girl who has been maladroit in her love-affairs instead of scheming to turn them to her own and her family's material profit. Thus Joan has a mean, calculating strain, and is entirely lacking in that refinement of mind which her daughter possesses in such a high degree. It is she, too, who most strongly presses the project of the visit to " The Slopes," though she has a momentary revulsion of feeling when Tess is actually starting out to take up her post there.

In addition to the disability of possessing parents like these, Tess is unlucky enough to be the first-born of a family of seven. Here and elsewhere [1] Hardy notes how mere multiplication is often an important factor in bringing about or prolonging a state of indigence. Even with a thrifty, hard-working and healthy father, a family of this size and in this economic grade would be brought up under severe disadvantages, but, with a head who is none of these things, the unfortunate young wayfarers start on their life's journey with the minimum of equipment to overcome the maximum of difficulty. And since Tess possesses an unselfish and conscientious mind, pure motives and strength of character, this state of affairs drives her into the position of leader. She has no one to look to for advice or assistance, and her responsibilities weigh heavily upon her. Indeed they are a contributory cause of her final disaster, and nothing could better demonstrate the closely knit character of Hardy's plots, the manner in which events follow one another in an inevitable sequence of cause and effect, than to trace this thread. First of all, she gives up two-thirds of the money, left for her by Clare, to thatch the Durbeyfield cottage, a piece of generosity which makes necessary her hard and bitter toil at Flintcomb-Ash. Then it is on her return to Flintcomb-Ash from Emminster (after an abortive visit to Clare's parents) that she re-encounters D'Urberville. Finally, the strongest weapon in the profligate's

[1] *E.g.* the Chickerels (*The Hand of Ethelberta*) and Mother Cuxsom's family (*The Mayor of Casterbridge*).

33

armoury at the last is his promise to benefit her family, now reduced to destitution through the death of John. Thus the conditions of Tess's home-life are the beginning of her sorrow and the culminating factor in bringing about her last and fatal surrender.

Jude comes upon the scene at the age of eleven years, and it is at once apparent that he is no ordinary boy, but a child full of ambition, possessing a preternatural solicitude for the animal world and an unusual insight for one so young. He lives in the care of his great-aunt, a baker, and from the first Hardy shows the conflict between the sensitive mind of Jude and the hard, narrow conditions under which his life is spent. He is " crazy for books," and consumed with desires and aspirations which those about him cannot understand, and which, moreover, coming to one in his penurious and orphaned state, lead his feet into rough and rugged pathways. He has this much in common with Tess, that he has hereditary tendencies to combat in addition to his other life-battles. Miss Fawley and Mrs Edlin are here used to give the impression that the Fawleys were not built for marriage, just as Clare is the mouthpiece of kindred ideas with reference to the D'Urbervilles, which seems to indicate that this point is one in which Hardy's own judgment is in suspension. It is pointed out in *The Return of the Native* that the transition from the bucolic to the intellectual stage usually takes place through the intermediary stage of social advancement. There would seem to be no deep-laid reason for the permanence of this condition, much of whose force is derived from long-standing social divisions and from the immemorial juxtaposition of rank and culture. The possibility of reform can only be properly examined in an age in which there is some approach to equality of opportunity in education. At all events, in Jude's day there is no escaping the struggle against adversity and indifference which bar his way towards academic distinction. Adversity alone would not have been insurmountable, but Jude is also face to face with a community recking little of learning and its ways and looking upon books as the preserve of a class other than their own, not to be approached by a baker's boy without his incurring the suspicion of being "stuck up." Nevertheless the baker's boy has unlimited ambition, perseverance and energy. In spite of all rebuffs he acquires a surprising amount of learning ; reading and translating with a pertinacity truly amazing and laudable, pursuing his task even in the old cart in which he delivers bread. His first serious set-back arises from causes other than his upbringing and home environment, and will be dealt with in a later chapter. In Jude's life up to his nineteenth year Hardy shows the clash of his temperament with poverty, lack of understanding in others, petty knavery like that of Vilbert, and entire absence of any guidance whatever. Had Jude not been poor, had he lived in other times, his career might have been very different. But Hardy only displays the "might-have-been" to show the imperfection of the "things that are."

It is a far cry from the supersensitive idealist, Jude, to the callous materialist, Dare (in *A Laodicean*), yet it is of interest to notice how the basic structures of their characters cause them to develop in very different ways under the pressure of circumstances not wholly dissimilar. Jude is an unwanted orphan and desires learning and distinction, Dare is an unwanted illegitimate child and desires money. The novel in which he appears, whether from the author's state of health at the time of writing or from other cause, is much slighter in significance than its immediate predecessors. In his preface of 1896 Hardy says it "may perhaps help to while away an idle afternoon. . . ." In that of 1912, with the remarkably sound faculty of self-criticism he so often shows, he ventures a modest hope for Paula, who is indeed not to be despised. *A Laodicean*, however, is nearer to the conventional novel of entanglement, *dénouement* and happy ending than any other of Hardy's books except the first, and Dare himself is in many respects a conventional figure, belonging to the line of Edmund in *King Lear*. It would be unjust to Hardy to suppose that he believes that "illegitimate" offspring are likely to be vicious simply because of their "illegitimacy." Coleridge has shown how the enormities of Edmund can be accounted for by the atmosphere in which he lived, and similarly from

36

the personality of de Stancy and from general reasoning we are able to draw some conclusions as to the forces which have made Dare what he is. Dare is thoroughly unprincipled. To him, honesty, far from being even the best policy, is merely an amiable weakness. There is something elf-like, savouring of "Gilpin Horner's brood" about his cunning and his sudden appearances where he is least desired or expected. He has the air of dancing round his victims, gloating over his own cleverness and their simplicity. The centre of all his schemes is his father, on whose fears and sentiments Dare plays with skill and pertinacity. Captain de Stancy is a thoroughgoing sentimentalist, and in the grip of his scheming, worldly-wise son is like clay in the hands of the potter ; for it frequently falls to the lot of sentimentalists to be directed and used by more practical natures, either for their good or, as in this case, to their undoing. Hardy gives no detailed account of Dare's life previous to his appearance at Stancy Castle, but the inference is that de Stancy has been a kind and probably a weakly indulgent father. This over-indulgence (proceeding from a mixture of fear and affection), together with the social disabilities and the too-early enlightenment as to the seamy side of life, which must be the portion of even the most favoured natural son, have produced their inevitable result. A child in Dare's position is bound to feel that life has been unjust to him, that he is suffering from no fault of his own. If, in addition to this, he possess a father who does not inspire respect, and if he be gifted with intelligence and ingenuity, he is likely to act as Dare acts, and endeavour to exploit the parent. In default of the usual training he is forced to fend for himself, and, since society blackballs him, he may retaliate by preying on the weaknesses of society. Dare, having come to this decision, rejects half-measures and proceeds pitilessly, with the utmost lack of scruple, using blackmail and forgery to further his ends. Havill is too weak to be a thorough rogue ; de Stancy, too, is troubled with qualms of conscience, and the manœuvre by which Dare secures his co-operation bears witness to that young man's perspicacity and power of reading character. It is the same low cunning which prompts him to conceal the expedients of the forged telegram and the " faked " photograph from the Captain, knowing that he would revolt against such depths of baseness. Dare remains unrepentant to the end, taking his defeat with jaunty impudence and utter unconcern for de Stancy's feelings. It is seldom that Hardy draws a character so consistent, and this very consistency takes away something of its verisimilitude ; but at the same time the figure of Dare has received less than justice at the critics' hands, for his parentage and position are skilfully combined with his inherent moral twist to produce a portrait by no means wholly improbable and unconvincing.

These three characters, Tess, Jude and Dare, are

those in which we most clearly discern Hardy's use of early surroundings and conditions as factors in the development of character. There are, of course, many other cases where the implication is present, but it is less clear and is overshadowed by larger issues. Stephen Smith's humble origin, with the difficulties to which it gives rise, Swithin St Cleeve's very similar circumstances, Elizabeth-Jane's quiet, hard-working childhood in a fishing village, at once come to mind. Manston [1] merits little attention, but it may be noticed that he, too, is an illegitimate child, wielding a great deal of power over his mother, though he is not so depraved as Dare (the killing of Mrs Manston is accidental, be it noted), and his ambitions take another direction. Cytherea and Owen Graye, in the same book,[1] are orphans, and very shiftless and innocent orphans indeed. Owen gives an impression of futility, and Cytherea, though charming in a doll-like way, allows herself to contract an alliance (after long cogitation about it) which she straightway repents. Much of this betrays the "'prentice hand": Owen's stilted conversation, Springrove's dramatic appearance at Cytherea's wedding, Manston's persistence in the marriage-project with a lady who calls him "Mr Manston," and his midnight adventure with the body in the sack, with three concealed watchers in attendance —all these things are evidences of immaturity over which it is needless to linger.

[1] *Desperate Remedies.*

Hardy almost invariably throws a backward glance at the days of youth from the point where he takes up the life-story of his most famous and closely studied personages. Angel Clare is contrasted with his two correct, conventional brothers, and yet, when Tess's confession comes, it becomes evident how very deeply the views of that Evangelical rectory, in which he has been brought up, have rooted themselves in his being, covered as they are with neo-pagan encrustations. Eustacia, too, never forgets Budmouth, with its bands, smart officers and gay parade of fashion. Grace Melbury and Clym Yeobright both feel the pull of their old environment, powerful in spite of all the changes of scene and interest they have undergone ; and Jocelyn Pierston, in his search for the Well-Beloved, comes back at the last to that strange island where he was born and where his imagination was fed with curious and fanciful lore.

CHAPTER II

LANDSCAPE, AND COUNTRY LIFE IN GENERAL

A STRONG characteristic of Hardy is the wide-awakeness of his senses to external impressions. An average intelligent observer notes small things and straightway forgets most of them, while the possessor of a highly trained memory retains a greater number in his mind, more or less isolated and disconnected. But an artist of Hardy's power not only absorbs minute details and changes in the world around him, but also links them up with human personality with consummate skill. His ears are open to every slight sound ; he sees (and makes *us* see) every delicate shade of colour, and he constantly creates the illusion in the reader's mind that he is in the actual spot described. We can see the dust rising up from the hot roadway, hear the rain's varying sound as it falls on different crops, mark the twisting and turning of leaves in a breeze, note the cloud closing " down upon the line of a distant ridge, like an upper upon a lower eyelid, shutting in the gaze of the evening sun." [1] His power of framing vivid and beautiful metaphors and similes has much to do with his

[1] *The Hand of Ethelberta*, p. 6.

success in reproducing impressions from without. There are ugly exceptions and occasional illustrations only to be understood by the technician (such as the " cima-recta or ogee " of Eustacia's mouth [1]), but for the most part they are telling and give that impression of utter rightness which alone stamps a simile or metaphor with success. This holds good even of the weaker novels, as a short passage from *The Hand of Ethelberta* will exemplify, especially in the last of the three metaphors : " . . . Her patent heels punched little D's in the soil with unerring accuracy wherever it was bare, crippled the heather-twigs where it was not, and sucked the swampy places with a sound of quick kisses." The weather and even the time of day and their effect on mood are included in his description. The strange, unearthly feeling of early morning to Clare in proximity to Tess, the tense, boding atmosphere while Gabriel Oak is working to save Bathsheba's ricks from coming storm, the sickly, garish appearance of the candle-lit ballroom when Ethelberta lets in the early sun's rays—these and many more scenes show natural aspects working on the mood of the personage and, through him or her, on that of the reader. There is, of course, nothing new in the attempt thus to reproduce atmosphere by working in scenic and atmospheric effects, but it has never been so successfully and strikingly carried out as by

[1] *The Return of the Native*, and *vide* Lionel Johnson, *op. cit.*, pp. 81-86.

Hardy. The natural features must not appear to be drawn in for effect as they do in John Galt, for example : the whole must be so arranged that the actors and their setting are absolutely co-ordinated, and that we could not imagine the one without the other; and this feeling of inevitableness is invariably produced by Hardy's work.

It is assisted by the general colouring of his outlook which pervades the novels—an outlook broad, comprehensive and taking in even the smaller creatures as well as the greater. What a quality of sympathy is evinced in the way he tells how, as the frost came on, " Many a small bird went to bed supperless that night among the bare boughs," [1] or how, with the advent of spring, " birds began not to mind getting wet." [2] Here it is playful and humorous ; but it often becomes charged with deep pathos, when the sorrows of the animal world are shown to be not less than our own, in proportion to their capacity for feeling :

> " And the poor beetle, that we tread upon,
>   In corporal sufferance finds a pang as great
>   As when a giant dies. . . ."

Tess, wounded in spirit, spends a night in a wood, and is melted to tears by the sufferings of the pheasants maimed in the interests of " sport," drawing a lesson from their plight with reference to her own :

[1] *Far from the Madding Crowd*, p. 22.
[2] *The Woodlanders*, p. 159.

43

"'Poor darlings — to suppose myself the most miserable being on earth in the sight o' such misery as yours!' she exclaimed, her tears running down as she killed the birds tenderly. 'And not a twinge of bodily pain about me! I be not mangled, and I be not bleeding, and I have two hands to feed and clothe me.' She was ashamed of herself for her gloom of the night, based on nothing more tangible than a sense of condemnation under an arbitrary law of society which had no foundation in Nature."

Sue Bridehead, a woman cast in a very different mould, is similarly sensitive to the appeal of her "weaker fellows in Nature's teeming family." She cannot bear the thought of her pigeons being slain by the poulterer, and impulsively releases them when opportunity offers. Both she and Jude are moved to put a trapped rabbit out of its misery, and Jude's extreme repugnance for the idea of inflicting pain emerges in his childish bird-scaring days and especially in the pig-killing incident, a piece of detailed horror which prompts the reflection that there would be many more vegetarians in the world if every man had to do his own slaughtering. The most moving of all Hardy's scenes in which animals play a leading part is that in which Fanny Robin, in the last stages of exhaustion, is helped to her refuge by a huge dog. This incident is portrayed with great fidelity to nature, and is not to be dismissed as improbable. Every person who knows and loves dogs will testify that they are quick to recognise and

44

sympathise with physical prostration in their human friends ; and just that touch of verisimilitude which finishes off the picture is added in the animal's inability to understand why Fanny sometimes sinks from his support. " The dog, who now thoroughly understood her desire and her incapacity, was frantic in his distress on these occasions ; he would tug at her dress and run forward." The reward dealt out to him by ironical Fate is such as is frequently meted out to the deserving :

" ' There is a dog outside,' murmured the overcome traveller. ' Where is he gone ? He helped me.'
" ' I stoned him away,' said the man."

Leaving these special aspects and returning to the general outlook on nature, we find several ways in which it is closely bound up with Hardy's technique. The first point is that Hardy is fond of beginning his stories with a road,[1] along which a pedestrian makes his way. Many of the novels and short stories commence in this manner, and it seems to set off humanity very well against the background of the earth, giving a peculiar feeling at the second reading —a feeling of privilege, because we now *know* that figure or those two or three figures who first appeared as mere specks in the midst of a vast champaign. It is at once uplifting and humbling to reflect that the mere hay-trusser who would have been seen

---

[1] S. C. Chew notices this (*op. cit.*, p. 122).

by a casual observer, doggedly walking to Weydon-Priors, and who is so unimportant in the scheme of things *qua* hay-trusser (or even *qua* Mayor), is nevertheless highly significant as a type of human character, wrong-headed, faulty, imprudent, it is true, but withal a " man of character "—that is to say, a man of principle and rugged determination. Again, the marvellous, Rembrandtesque picture of Egdon Heath unfolds itself before us with its white road bisecting it and intensifying its solitude ; and then, crawling like a fly over this huge heath, older than the seas, comes the figure of Captain Vye. To the Heath, and to the world, Vye and Venn with his cart and its burden are but accidental, temporary things which happen to be there at the moment. Then, as the story unfolds itself, we find that Venn and Thomasin, and above all the daughter of Vye, are related to the Heath in a very close fashion by bonds of love or bonds of hatred and imprisonment.

Another very striking technical device of Hardy's is to begin a chapter with a paragraph relating the state of the country and its changes due to the weather and the time of the year. This method gives a sense of reality and continuity that would be difficult to match in any fiction. It is most apparent in *The Woodlanders* and creates the illusion of living in the spot described and marking the rolling seasons in their course, the more skilful in its artistry because in real life these changes occur

46

gradually and without noticeable gradations.[1] But they do undoubtedly affect the mind and mood of humanity, usually in an imperceptible way, and it is the mark of a very high art that it opens the mind to the significance of such things and gives unity to a series of incoherent impressions.

The third and greatest characteristic of Hardy's treatment of the world of natural things (comprehending the other two, but containing something more) is the implication that the scene is not merely passive, but is an actor in the human drama. Sir Walter Raleigh writes of Wordsworth : " His stage was bare of scenery, and held nothing but the actors," and in a sense this is true of Hardy. The word " scenery " has to be used because there is no substitute for it, but it is misleading when referred to the Wessex Novels, unless it be clearly understood to mean something which is not *outside* the drama of existence—existence for all things consisting in growth and conflict followed by a sudden cutting-off or slow decay. Again, as in Wordsworth, there is a certain pantheism to be detected in Hardy's thought, a feeling that all things are the children of Earth and bound up with her life ; but with the novelist this does not lead to optimism or belief in the beneficence of nature. Wordsworth expressed his point of view in casting his memory back over Cambridge days, when :

[1] J. W. Beach (*The Technique of Thomas Hardy*, p. 167) falls foul of this.

47

CHARACTER AND ENVIRONMENT

" To every natural form, rock, fruit or flower,
Even the loose stones that cover the highway,
I gave a moral life : I saw them feel,
Or linked them to some feeling. . . ." [1]

A recent critic, Mr H. C. Duffin, deals with the
difference between these two great ones in nature-
lore by saying :

" Hardy nowhere expresses the extreme inference
' that every flower enjoys the air it breathes.' For
the definite formulation and acceptance of that faith
perhaps the more transcendent vision of the poet is
required." [2]

Now, in the first place, the same thought occurred
to that very logical and unpoetical person, Samuel
Butler, and was developed by him at some length
in *Erewhon*. Secondly, it is strange to read any
implication of a want of poetic vision on the part
of the author of Marty's lament over the grave of
Giles or the passage on Tess listening to Clare's
harp, to cite two out of a thousand prose poems.
Putting aside the " vulgar error," as Shelley calls
it, of requiring verse as an indispensable concomitant
of poetry, and considering Hardy's work as a whole,
it will be found that in reach of imagination, in
beauty of language and simile, in vivid and telling
expression of deep emotion, his prose is superior to
his verse. But even were this not so, the real reason
for Hardy's divergence from Wordsworth's track of

[1] *The Prelude*, Book 3.   [2] *Thomas Hardy*, 1921, p. 57.

thought lies in something other than the measure of
his poetic gift. Up to a point the two writers go
hand in hand. Both love the open life among the
country solitudes, and feel and convey the beauty of
nature's external aspects. Both admire the simple,
rustic people who dwell far from towns. Both link
up all life in one great family proceeding from the
Mother Earth. But on "nature's holy plan" and
on "trailing clouds of glory" Hardy pours out his
scorn. Nature is beautiful, yes, but she is the hapless
instrument of blind law, and, as such, he is as much
convinced of her non-morality as Huxley was. In
the Hintock Woods, "the Unfulfilled Intention,
which makes life what it is, was as obvious as it
could be among the depraved crowds of a city slum.
The leaf was deformed, the curve was crippled, the
taper was interrupted ; the lichen ate the vigour
of the stalk, and the ivy slowly strangled to death
the promising sapling." [1] So that, though nature's
beauty may be a refuge and a solace to percipient
man, he must forget these things for the time if
he is to benefit.

Frequent use of similes from living things serves
to deepen this sense of the inanimate as a personality.
At Tess's confession the very furniture of the room
takes on a mocking aspect, and when all is over the
indifferent night swallows up the happiness of Clare.
The sea enters into several novels and short stories,
and has received less attention from the critics than

[1] *The Woodlanders*, p. 59.

it deserves. Even its sound is connected with animal life by such a simile as the following : "The hissing fleece of froth slid again down the shingle, dragging the pebbles under it with a rattle as of a beast gnawing bones." [1] The bitter, upland farm at Flintcomb-Ash, where Tess spends a winter, has a bare field like a " brown face " confronting the " white face " of the sky above.

Small as is the region with which Hardy is mainly concerned, the aerial quality of his vision lifts us above the earth like one of the spirits in his own epic-drama, so that we see human life at once in the light of the universal and the particular, in a manner that no ranging abroad after " local colour " could equal. Gabriel Oak on Norcombe Hill in the small hours can almost feel the movement of the earth on its axis. Swithin St Cleeve powerfully demonstrates the awfulness and immensity of space, but at length finds, with Viviette, that mundane things are more pressing and powerful. Thus does Hardy " set the emotional history of two infinitesimal lives against the stupendous background of the stellar universe ; . . . to impart to readers the sentiment that of these contrasting magnitudes the smaller might be the greater to them as men." [2] In that " might " lurks a world of irony, the irony of the importance of the small in those " infinitesimal lives " which, through the growth of percipience, have become subject to

[1] *The Hand of Ethelberta*, p. 386.
[2] *Two on a Tower* (Preface).

new desires which are at variance with the laws of the rest of creation.

Hardy's method of representing the features of field, wood and dale is by an accumulation of minute but relevant detail. Liberal as this piling-up of detail is, it is seldom prodigal, seldom felt to be superfluous. For one thing he never loses much time before bringing his actors on the stage and starting the action on its way. Many readers find the mass of detail in scenery, costume and history with which Scott frequently begins his books wearisome and uninteresting, largely because it is at the beginning, before their interest in the characters has been aroused. Hardy at most interposes a chapter between the reader and the first movements of the human beings who are to be followed, and similarly begins his description of these people with a page or two only. Afterwards, in the course of the narrative, he adds many touches to both landscape and portraiture, and stops (usually at the commencement of a chapter) to describe a new scene or a building, or to reflect generally on some aspect of affairs at the stage at which they have arrived. As he does not fall into the error of making these lulls the occasion for long moral discourses, they give an impression of stateliness and breadth—qualities which are indeed strongly marked in all the serious portions of Hardy's writings, and which are assisted by the dignity of his descriptive prose. Upon close consideration of the prose style (apart from rustic dialect and some playfully satirical

passages) it becomes evident that Hardy's main
effort in this direction has been to secure the word
which most clearly and exactly conveys a meaning
to himself, even though it be drawn from technical
or scientific diction. He is never afraid of using
"hard" words, and his temerity in this respect sometimes leads him into harshness, and into the usage of
images and terms which no layman of reasonable
education could be expected to comprehend. Even
if readily comprehensible, these images are at times
far-fetched and anything but felicitous. Thus of a
certain lady he says : "Her virtues lay in no resist-
ant force of character, but in a natural inappetency
for evil things, *which to her were as unmeaning as
joints of flesh to a herbivorous creature*." [1] And
there is something heavy in applying such a word as
"thesmothete" to Bathsheba, even in a scene where
she has exhibited all the qualities indicated thereby.

It is this fondness for technical terms which
renders Hardy's descriptions of buildings less striking and effective than those of natural things. He
was never a professional botanist (though even here
he falls, on occasion, as when he alludes, in *The
Return of the Native*, chapter vii., to "a prickly
tuft of the large *Ulex Europæus*"), but he was for
years a professional architect, and at times cannot
resist the temptation to import into his novels some
of the phraseology learnt in his early calling. The
shearing-barn in *Far from the Madding Crowd* is

[1] *A Group of Noble Dames* (Dame 9). (Italics mine.)

52

marked by only two or three of these architectural terms, such as "collars," "lanceolate windows" and "chamfers." He has never lost interest in architecture as a study, and can even draw material for satire out of it in such a passage as that describing Lord Mountclere's house, which, though built of brick, is carefully faced with stucco to give the appearance of solid stone. Buildings again are given a personality. The aforementioned shearing-barn, unlike the neighbouring and contemporary church and castle, is still used for the purpose which has dictated its erection in mediæval times, and refers to " no exploded fortifying art or worn-out religious creed. The defence and salvation of the body by daily bread is still a study, a religion, and a desire." The same idea appears in *Tess* with reference to the abbey and the mill, near that grim old house of the D'Urbervilles, whose panel-portraits strike such a chill of ill-omen into the heart of Tess. The Christminster colleges are presented rather by broad strokes than in detail, serving to call up in Jude's mind the hosts of sages and poets who in past years have lived within their walls. Stancy Castle presides over the story of *A Laodicean* as an ever-present influence, recalling (though *very* faintly) that other overshadowing presence—Egdon Heath.

The name Egdon Heath conjures up that most queenly of Hardy's heroines, Eustacia Vye, whose history embodies in its clearest and fullest form the idea of environment as a very large factor in the shaping of character. It has been already postulated that those characters in the Wessex Novels are on the whole most placid and contented who chance to live their lives in a favourable environment. Paula Power, in a letter, enunciates another aspect of this view when she states her belief in hoping for and expecting the best : " My opinion is that, to be happy, it is best to think that, as we are the products of events, events will continue to produce that which is in harmony with us." [1] This gospel of cheerfulness and hope for the best conforms to the teaching of old moralists and modern scientists ; but it has been by many found easier to advise than to practise. The mischief is that mere cheerfulness is so frequently the result of lack of imagination and ignorance of the real conditions of life. Of Eustacia a superficial judge might make a very rough and hostile summing-up—that she was an indolent, conceited and discontented woman, who, with no real troubles, created factitious ones for herself and other people. The ordinary woman, he might say, would have found something to occupy her mind, and "made the best of things." But then "ordinary" people—that is to say, average people—are no fit subjects for great drama.[2] Eustacia, from her first

[1] *A Laodicean*, p. 300.

[2] *Cf.* R. A. Scott-James, *Modernism and Romance*, 1908, chap. v. Hardy takes as his leading figures, "fully developed characters, sensitive to impressions, capable of cherishing some sort of personal ideal and of being prostrated by the unintelligible cruelty of their lot."

appearance on the scene, is found to be very far removed from the average. *The Return of the Native* begins with a picture of Egdon Heath, a passage of prose which, by general consent, is the finest ever produced by Hardy. Ancient, unchanging, untamable, sombre and tremendous, the Heath is painted with the brush of a master, not feature by feature, but in a series of bold sweeps. No fact is too small and none too great to contribute to this prelude—the furze-cutter's sense of the November afternoon there is succeeded by the poet's sense of Egdon awaiting, through centuries, the end of the world. It is in accord with moods of loneliness, melancholy and even tragedy, and these moods predominate in the nature of its adopted child, Eustacia. She is first seen through the eyes of Venn, standing upon an ancient barrow surmounting the highest hill, distant, motionless, and in keeping, so that her shape indeed seems part of the landscape. After this brief glimpse from a distance she is dismissed for some chapters, but when she reappears it is to dominate the whole book.

The dominant figures in most of the Wessex Novels are women, but on none of them except Tess has the author spent so much energy and skill as on the portrait of Eustacia. The method employed in describing her shows that she is intended to be taken very seriously, as a study of strong but abnormal personality, and by no means a mere

55

vulgar butterfly, pining for frivolity at any cost. The " Queen of Night " chapter deserves to rank with the Egdon chapter in imaginative power of delineation. Having once read it, we return to it again and again to gaze, with the mind's eye, on this rare, dark, beautiful, intense creature, whose hair closes " over her forehead like nightfall extinguishing the western glow." " Her presence brought memories of such things as Bourbon roses, rubies, and tropical midnights ; her moods recalled lotus-eaters and the march in *Athalie* ; her motions, the ebb and flow of the sea ; her voice, the viola." [1] Responsive to out-of-the-way sensuous impressions, careless of conventions, dignified, and hating her enforced loneliness, she lives on, ever waiting for some experience, the nature of which she hardly knows, except that love shall form a part of it. Hers is the tragedy of unrealised (and scarcely visualised) aspirations. As a woman she is absolutely at variance with her surroundings : as an artistic creation she is triumphantly akin to them, and her very rebellion, in all its ineffectiveness, only serves to show up the grandeur and malign force of the Heath which forms her prison. Waiting for the great love, she makes shift with Wildeve for a time, and yet knows that he reigns only because of the lack of anyone more worthy. When Yeobright returns to Egdon, Eustacia, after seeing him by the freakish and unconventional device of going to the house with the

[1] *The Return of the Native*, p. 76.

mummers, fixes on him as a greater than Wildeve, and their courtship and marriage follow.

The semi-blindness of Clym is the last blow to all Eustacia's hopes of escape from Egdon. She has known that Clym intends to keep a school, but has trusted to her womanly persuasion to divert him from the project ; and his misfortune adds one more burden to those she already bears. Clym's cheerfulness under privation, which would have been heroic had he only had himself to consider, amounts almost to callousness where Eustacia is concerned. It is small wonder that she is grieved and angry when he takes his fall (which involves hers) complacently. For the conduct of Mrs Yeobright there is even less excuse. Her heart-rending journey in the burning heat to Alderworth, her return thence, exhausted and heart-broken, so well brought out by the conversation with Johnny, her natural motherly grief at what she supposes is a brutal rebuff on the part of Clym and his wife, her tragic fate from the bite of an adder—these excite our compassion very strongly. But she is intolerant and hot-tempered, possessing an unhappy capacity for " rubbing people up the wrong way," as shown by her theatrical forbidding of Thomasin's banns, her tactless way of opposing Clym's schemes, and her unwarrantable acrimony and unpardonable accusations against Eustacia. Clym's accusations are even more coarse and equally groundless, and in both these superb quarrel scenes the sympathies of one reader at least are unreservedly

57

with Eustacia. But both Yeobright and his mother, in their anger, know only half, or a quarter, of the truth. All three are close-gripped in the meshes of destiny. Clym has failed to find peace abroad, and returns to seek it in his native wilds, only to become enamoured of one who craves for the life he despises and who hates the land in which circumstance has decreed she shall spend her days. And instead of a catalyser to aid in the fusion of these two opposites, there is the disturbing, unreasonable, intractable Mrs Yeobright, whose interference causes fresh misery and brings about her own pathetic end.

Wildeve, like Eustacia, is an alien on the Heath. His outward mien and bearing are impressed at once on the memory by one of those epigrammatic touches which are not so rare in Hardy's work as is generally supposed : " Altogether he was one in whom no man would have seen anything to admire, and in whom no woman would have seen anything to dislike." He has at one time been an engineer, but, failing in that profession, has become the landlord of the " Quiet Woman " inn at Blooms-End, and it is hinted that this fall is due to a weakness of character. He trims for a long time between Thomasin and Eustacia, and the greater of these feminine forces draws him like a magnet even after he has married the lesser—largely out of pique. He has all the instincts of a lady-killer, and lacks the moral force to leave Eustacia undisturbed when both of them have married elsewhere and so made lawful relationship impossible. After the rupture between Eustacia and Clym and the sudden access of Wildeve to wealth, he forms a last hope in Eustacia's mind of escaping from the Heath. He gladly leaves it at the first opportunity, and, quite indifferent to Thomasin's feelings, is preparing to take Eustacia with him, when the opportunity occurs for him to show a streak of nobility. The manner in which he rises to the occasion, leaping into the dark, boiling weir, without even removing his greatcoat, to the rescue of Eustacia, almost redeems his other faults ; and at least, if he has committed many paltry actions, he dies like a hero.

If Eustacia and Wildeve are types upon which the lonely solemnity of Egdon presses like an incubus, Thomasin and Venn are undismayed by it. They are simpler natures, whose spiritual and emotional needs are satisfied even in this grim place, and the desire for the intellectual and social movement of town circles has no part in their lives. Thomasin is not one of those figures whose image stamps itself indelibly on the memory. She may be classed rather with Elizabeth-Jane, Anne Garland and Picotee than with Eustacia, Sue and Ethelberta. The first three attract by their simplicity, ingenuousness and native goodness of heart, their qualities of mind being mainly passive and negative : they are the primroses in the Wessex garden. The second three, though not possessing the gentler, more childlike virtues, have something dynamic in their composition and something not altogether virtuous, yet they are more highly developed, and there is satisfaction for the reader in their very discontent and all it connotes. Thomasin's path is the way of submission ; she submits to Mrs Yeobright, to Wildeve, and to her immediate physical surroundings, and in consequence, though she has sufferings they never reach tragic pitch. She is clearly aware, after her marriage, that all is not over between Wildeve and Eustacia, but the part she plays is not one of indignation or recrimination but of gentle forbearance and absorption in the business of her home. She is a lovable but quite prosaic personality ; " a primrose by a river's brim " is a yellow primrose to her, and nothing more. Her reflections as she walks through the rain on the night of disaster contain no feeling of the Heath as a personality; she neither loves its moods with Clym nor hates them with Eustacia. " At this time it was in her view a windy, wet place, in which a person might experience much discomfort, lose the path without care, and possibly catch cold."

Diggory Venn has been placed alongside Oak and Winterborne as an embodiment of the best features of rural manhood and simplicity ; but he stands somewhat apart from these two, both in temperament and in the part he plays in the action of *The Return of the Native*. Oak and Winterborne are so inevitably bound up with the dramas in which they participate that the stories could not be imagined without them. Venn, too, is a thread of importance in the closely woven fabric of *The Return* : as far as its present plot goes, he is indispensable, but the interest of the general situation is not greatly increased by his presence, for his marriage with Thomasin at the end was added only to please the magazine-public, and there can be small question that the real ending of the tale should be at the close of Book 5. But apart from the unbelievable way in which he always appears on the scene at opportune moments, he is definitely below Oak and Winterborne as a specimen of manhood. His force of quiet affection, his simplicity, his unselfishness are akin to theirs, but we could not imagine either of them playing the deliberate part of eavesdropper as Venn continually does. He is working in a good cause, and the unselfishness of his love is shown by his efforts to persuade Eustacia to relinquish her hold on Wildeve, when a union of these two might well have worked to Venn's advantage. But there is no escaping the fact that he is a very thoroughgoing spy, and spies, in whatever cause, are never very desirable persons. Like Thomasin, he knows the Heath thoroughly, and it has no terrors for him, either of a practical or an imaginative kind. He is not so plain and direct in his ways as are most of Hardy's countrymen, for he is capable of employing subterfuge in support of his aims, and displays a grim, satirical turn of mind on occasion. After seeing Wildeve part from Eustacia on the night of the "gipsying," he interviews Thomasin ; and, learning that Wildeve has been to buy a horse— "'Then I saw him at Throope Corner, leading one home,' said Venn drily. 'A beauty, with a white face and a mane as black as night.'"

A significant fact with reference to the principal countrymen in the novels of Hardy is that their preeminent qualities are a deep-seated stoicism coupled with the most intense reserve. These characteristics are what he admires most in a man, while he is not attracted to intellectual brilliance alone, and still less to the showy and flamboyant. This attitude is a natural corollary of his general attitude towards life, which seems to him a losing battle against indifferent but powerful forces. The noblest nature, as he conceives it, is the one which never gives way to cowardly shrinking nor thoughtless abandon, but, dimly realising the seriousness of the conflict, continues to struggle, and remains unbending under the hard blows of fate. Reserve, too, he naturally admires, for the bravest men are those who, far from glorying in their bravery, are hardly conscious of it. More generally, reserve is a component of the greatest art, and how well Hardy himself practises it his handling of delicate situations bears witness. This strength of character, it is implied, is drawn up from the soil by those who live in close contact therewith. The sophisticated man is almost invariably less noble than his unsophisticated brother in the Wessex Novels. Farfrae is perhaps the only one among them for whom we are not impelled to qualify very seriously our admiration. This point is one on which many will find it hard to see eye to eye with Hardy. In one place he speaks of " how little acquirements and culture weigh beside sterling personal character," [1] which will be readily conceded if " culture " be taken in the sense of erudition alone. But surely this is an arbitrary narrowing-down of the term. Culture, rightly apprehended, should *include* high personal character with a great many qualities of mind superadded. To deny the worth of true culture (as distinguished from mere cleverness) is a retrograde proceeding which, if pushed to its logical conclusion, leads to the flagrant heresy propagated by the school of Rousseau—that the savage is the ideal man and that civilisation is pernicious. To this there can be only one answer.

But, from a close examination of the novel in which this attitude is most clearly expressed, it can be shown that Winterborne, though not in the full sense a cultured man, has attributes which constitute him a gentleman in the best meaning of that much-abused word. Hardy's life has been spent among rural folk, and his writings have, among other things, been directed to show that " the pitiable dummy known as Hodge " [2] is a figment of the townsman's imagination. On the other hand it is questionable whether he has not gone to the opposite extreme, and cast an idealising veil over the grosser side of the

[1] *The Woodlanders*, p. 404.   [2] *Tess*, p. 152.

simple countryman. Such idealisation is no doubt necessary in art, and it would be a foolish seeker who hoped to find in every milkmaid the soul of a Tess. A paragraph describing Winterborne's state of mind after the *faux pas* of taking Grace to lunch at a shoddy inn throws a strong light on his character :

" He feared anew that they could never be happy together, even should she be free to choose him. She was accomplished : he was unrefined. It was the original difficulty, which he was too thoughtful to recklessly ignore, as some men would have done in his place." [1]

From this it will be observed that Winterborne *realises* his own deficiencies, and realisation, in a case like this, is half way to correction. No completely vulgar person has the faintest suspicion that he is vulgar, just as no complete lunatic suspects that he is insane : indeed a total blindness to all the finer shades and meanings of life is the salient symptom of vulgarity. Winterborne, whether as a woodman or as a cider-maker, is the product of the country in which he lives. Marty South is closely associated with him in his work, and her thoughts and comments help to amplify the description of him. The picture which shows him as " Autumn's very brother," walking with Grace behind his apple-mill, has the rich brown tones and the luminosity of a work by Millet. He can plant saplings with unerring skill ; he can fell trees or make cider, and

[1] *The Woodlanders*, p. 345.

is at home in the woods at all times and seasons. His life is a solitary one, and this helps to develop in him the quiet dignity with which he is invested, for a rural existence of this kind is very different from one which includes fraternising with other villagers at the inn and elsewhere. Melbury's vow of reparation to the Winterborne family by giving Grace to Giles in marriage puts him into a position of great difficulty. But when he brings Grace home from Sherton Abbas his approach to her on the vital subject is delicate enough, and shows that whatever roughnesses of manner he may possess, they are overshadowed by his great chivalry. He is modest and unselfish too : he does not storm or bluster when Melbury revokes his promise, but quietly relinquishes his claim to Grace, and preserves an attitude of admirable restraint all through the time of Grace's courtship and marriage to Fitzpiers. In loyalty, affection and integrity there can be no doubt of his fitness for Grace, but his woodland ways tell heavily against him, as, in this world, small things do often tell against greater. The party he gives, with all the will in the world to please the Melburys, is a total failure on account of his social shortcomings. He begins by giving them an off-hand invitation, so that they arrive too soon ; his boy smears the chairs with greasy furniture-polish ; his man serves a certain dish by turning its contents bodily into a platter, so that hot splashes rise up at the guests. Then the cards are thumbed and stained, the dancing is

65

old-fashioned and unknown to Grace, and, to crown all, the ears of the Melburys are offended, as they walk homewards, by hearing from the lips of two of the guests the strains of a ribald song.

In the everyday petty intercourse of society, manners often seem to matter more than morals, because our ordinary relationships with acquaintances are not such as to touch the deeper strata where moral valuations come into question. Hence at this early stage of his courtship, when his fate still hangs in the balance and when Grace has not yet reverted to her love of the simple life, Winterborne's party does much to turn the scale against him. Fate steps in with the death of John South, and Winterborne's consequent loss of his copyhold house. Even this might have been averted but that he has hardened Mrs Charmond's heart against him by impeding with his wagon the progress of her carriage—a piece of churlishness out of accord with his nature and caused by temporary pique at the sex after an interview with Grace the previous day. Through all the course of Fitzpiers's *liaison* with Mrs Charmond, and the gradual suspicion, ripening into certitude, of Grace and Melbury, Giles seldom appears. He has temporarily dropped out of the picture. But in Grace's mind a revulsion of feeling is taking place, and, with the revival of her interest in Giles and the growth of her admiration for his deeper qualities, there goes a corresponding diminution in her aversion to his superficial ruggedness.

When hopes for divorce run high, and Grace is counselled by her father and by her own feelings to be kind to Winterborne, he commits his single lapse from the strict restraint which has hitherto bound him. It is, however, natural and excusable ; and it is forgotten in that last great act of self-sacrifice and devotion, when the woodsman gives up his very life rather than compromise Grace.

In thus bringing about the death of Winterborne, Hardy does the one possible thing to make us accept this character at the valuation he puts on it. The tragic scenes in the forest invest Winterborne with a saintly halo, and forbid us from carping criticism. But to say that the character is well-balanced, thoroughly rationalised and true to life is another matter. We have only to imagine Grace and Giles married to realise the absolute disaster such a union would have been. It is incredible that the well-nurtured Grace would have been anything but unhappy with a mate who, however affectionate, lived in a totally different intellectual world.

Marty South takes a subordinate place in *The Woodlanders*, but she is unforgettable by reason of the pathos of her lot and the simple fidelity of her affection for Winterborne. Like him, she is the child of the woods, knowing the lore of trees and birds, and living a quiet life of ill-paid toil at hard, manual tasks. She, too, is a poetic and romantic figure, and no more a typical country-girl than Winterborne is a typical woodsman. A number of

67

pictures of Marty are fit to go alongside that of
" Autumn's brother." Such are the first, when she
is discovered making spars ; the vigil after her
father's death ; and the last, at the end of the book,
wherein she stands at the grave of Giles and makes
her lament.

These two, with Gabriel Oak, represent Hardy's
conception of the rural character at its best. Oak,
however, displays, in even higher degree than
Winterborne, an absolute mastery of his daily work
and absorption therein, so that he falls most naturally into the later chapter dealing with the influence
of occupations. It remains to consider the dark side
of rural character, in its most typical representative.
Of course the whole of Hardy's work is impregnated
with the flavour of the earth, and the fact of living
in close contact with untamed nature is an important factor in the lives of nearly all his personages ;
and therefore this chapter must confine itself to
those cases where this seems to have been the most
powerful environmental agency.

To the devotee of what Carlyle called
" Werterism," and even to a much less sentimental
inquirer, it might seem natural that a life removed
from the manifold temptations of the city should
always be the purest and best. Looking upon the
grim solemnity of a Cader Idris or upon the ideally
peaceful and proportionate combination of sea, hill
and woodland of a Donegal, it is sometimes difficult
to believe but that such scenes exercise an ennobling

influence on those who dwell among them. Some such feeling as this is bound up in Hardy's frequent ascription of the highest nobility to simple characters. None the less he has shown, in many minor peasant figures and in one of first importance to his latest novel (*Jude the Obscure*), that he recognises that country isolation, in some natures, results not in ennoblement, but in almost unrestrained animalism. The villager is nearer to the primitive state than his brother of the town : convention presses less heavily upon him, and he cares less for public opinion of his conduct. These and kindred causes produce a general loosening of behaviour, and the academic seeker after Strephons and Corydons is thus apt to receive a severe shock when he comes to look closely into village morality. Natures which thus relapse are, of course, no fit subjects for the principal actors in great drama, and hence Hardy generally passes lightly over them. But he is not blind to all this : numerous instances of irregularities of varying shades of darkness could be collected from the Wessex Novels and tales, and it is only necessary to recall Suke Damson (in *The Woodlanders*) and Mop Ollamoor (in *Life's Little Ironies*) as exemplars. A character, however, much more closely studied, and playing a much larger part in the action of *Jude* than Suke does in that of *The Woodlanders*, is Arabella Donn.

It has been remarked by Mr S. C. Chew and others that Hardy chooses his surnames with an eye to their suitability for their bearers, just as Le Sage,

69

Fielding, Sheridan and Dickens did. The aptness
of such patronymics as Oak and Henchard, with
their respective flavours of sturdy strength and
dogged determination, is obvious, and surely it is no
wayward fancy to see something singularly fitting in
both the Christian and surname of Arabella Donn.
In the life of Jude she represents profane love in
contradistinction to Sue, who typifies the sacred.
The means whereby she first attracts his attention
are in keeping with her conduct throughout, which
remains fairly consistent. She is thoroughly coarse
and brutish, and sets out, by hook or by crook, to
marry Jude (as the most presentable young man who
has yet crossed her path), attaining this end first by
pandering to the baser side of his nature and then
by deceiving him on a vital point. His speedy disillusionment arouses in her nothing but scorn ; their
quarrel develops into the most sordid of brawls, and
ends by Arabella's departure for Australia. It has
already been shown that she has the contempt of
the thoroughly vulgar and ignorant for Jude's aspirations and his learning. The last intolerable thing is
Jude's discovery that even his signed photograph has
been sold at the auction of the household goods.
There is no trace of true and spiritual love here!
When she comes a second time into his ken, her
absolute lack of delicacy is even more strongly
marked by her inability to understand Jude's indignation at her concealment of the bigamous union
with Cartlett. This worthy is shortly but vigorously

sketched, and appears as a disgusting contrast to Jude, showing how far Arabella is capable of sinking—"a short, rather bloated man, with a globular stomach and small legs, resembling a top on two pegs."[1] It is to marry this person and share his public-house in Lambeth, "that excellent, densely populated, gin-drinking neighbourhood," that she obtains her divorce. Seeing Jude and Sue together, she begins to envy their happiness (and, incidentally, sums up Sue's feelings towards him pretty shrewdly), and in the end recaptures his body, though she could never reach his soul. This woman is the worst kind which the countryside brings forth, driven into scheming and every kind of baseness by poverty, ignorance and bad example. The moral standpoint of her parents and friends is like that of Joan Durbeyfield—"if he don't marry her afore he will after."[2] It is good that Hardy has delineated this sorry character, in the interests of truth, but it is good also that he has for the most part preferred to expend his resources not on the weeds but on the more rare and beautiful flowers that grow in the garden of Wessex.

[1] *Jude*, p. 350.   [2] *Tess*, p. 61.

CHAPTER III

MANNERS, CUSTOMS AND SUPERSTITIONS
OF THE WESSEX PEASANTS

SOME attempt was made in the last chapter to examine Hardy's attitude towards nature and his method of dealing with landscape, and also to show the way in which some of his more prominent characters are influenced, for good or evil, by their immediate physical surroundings. Apart from these principal figures, however, which Hardy places in the foreground, the Wessex Novels contain a body of subordinates who are indispensable as parts of the picture—the peasants, among whom the author has spent most of his life, and whose idiosyncrasies and naïve demeanour he delights to depict. These labourers, " to whom labour suggests nothing more than a wrestle with gravitation, and pleasure nothing better than a renunciation of the same," [1] are of a type fast disappearing during the twenty-seven years in which the novels were issued, and now, no doubt, well-nigh passed away completely. In the Preface to the 1895 edition of *Far from the Madding Crowd* Hardy remarks the gradual change from the

[1] *Far from the Madding Crowd*, p. 43.

72

conditions he describes, putting it down largely to the substitution of migratory labour for the old state of affairs under which son followed father in the one village for generations. In the same place he notes that the success of his adoption of the old word "Wessex" has been beyond his expectations, and warns readers that, though it is applicable to the particular part of southern England with which he is mainly concerned, it is more properly reserved for his own special artistic world—"the horizons and landscapes of a partly real, partly dream-country." In other prefaces to the later editions he throws out a few hints to "scene-hunters," but often reminds them that transferences of buildings have been made and that regions which are portrayed in the various novels have been built up from features belonging to a number of separate places. Mr Sherren (in *The Wessex of Romance*) and others have identified Hardy's place-names with the real ones and shown how he has not invented them arbitrarily, but has chosen words in keeping with the character of the original name. Sometimes they are slight variations from the original (as, for example, Kingsbere for Bere Regis) and sometimes he translates into the name the spirit of the town, as in Christminster (Oxford) or Quartershot (Aldershot).

These warnings against judging the Wessex Novels on a too-literal basis of fidelity to actual outward appearance are only necessary for those who expect from a territorial writer a "Handbook

to the scenery, folk-lore and customs " of certain
counties. To those who look for these things
rather as ingredients of an art occupying itself with
aspects of art's eternal subject—human life—it will
not appear as a defect that the peasants, though
not glorified, are in some measure idealised.[1] They
strike, none the less, a true note, and the highest
praise that can be meted out to them is that they re-
semble the rustics of Shakespeare—a likeness that has
been observed by many critics of Hardy. In depict-
ing them, no less than the principal actors, Hardy
shows them as the product of the conditions under
which they live. All those forces which in towns
tend to reduce the manual worker to the status of a
machine, all those educative influences which tend
to make him a thinker and destroy his naïveté, have
(in the time of which Hardy writes) not yet been
brought to bear on the children of Wessex. His
point of view is so modern that we are apt to forget
that he is dealing with the England of mid-Victorian
days until we are stopped short by some passage
which emphasises it, such as Angel Clare's feeling
of oddness (quite comic and French in this century)
that he is allowed to walk abroad with his betrothed
without supervision or shock to the conventions.
Hardy was born in Dorsetshire, and, as has been
said, has spent most of his life there, and so knows
the rural nature well, and exhibits it in the light

[1] It should be said that Mr Duffin notes this idealisation
(*op. cit.*, p. 19).

74

of prevalent customs, folk-lore and superstitions in a
way which shows the thorough mastery of medium
rarely attained by any other than a native.

The conversations of the rustics give scope for
a rich humour which plays about them, venting itself in short descriptive " asides " or gently ironical
comments on the part of the author, making these
scenes a welcome relief to the sad " twilight " [1]
tinge predominating in most of the books. Dialogue
between educated persons is noticeably formal and
far enough removed from " the real language of
men," but a too faithful realism in this respect
would be tedious. Nine out of ten real conversations
are desultory, *décousues* and full of phrases thrown
in by the auditor in order to show that he is atten-
tive ; and therefore the selective judgment must be
exercised in reproducing them. The rustic talk is
more convincing, and it is but rarely that we find an
uneducated man using a phrase out of keeping with
his status ; though there are occasional instances of
this, as, for example, when Sol Chickerel says " will
answer my purpose " instead of the more likely " will
suit me " or " will do for me." [2] But in general the
humble folk speak a language which gives the effect
of *patois* without any attempt at phonetic spelling
on the author's part, and with only a sparing introduction of contractions and dialectic expressions
(such as " en," for the accusative singular personal

[1] George Meredith writes of Hardy's "twilight view of life."
[2] *The Hand of Ethelberta*, p. 420.

pronoun; " home-along" and the rest). There is an old-world, semi-Biblical strain in it, difficult to define, but triumphantly conveying the effect of rich dialect. Hardy clearly loves this old tongue, and has a serio-comic passage in *The Mayor of Casterbridge*, where the successful corn-merchant chides his daughter for saying " Bide where you be " instead of " Stay where you are." " The sharp reprimand was not lost upon her, and in time it came to pass that for ' fay ' she said ' succeed '; that she no longer spoke of ' dumbledores ' but of ' humble bees ' . . ." [1] Not only is Hardy attached to the quaint speech of the people, but he clearly feels that education (at all events of the council-school kind) robs them of much picturesqueness without replacing it by anything worth having. So strong is this feeling that it is impossible to appraise his treatment of peasant character without taking it into account, and in Pierston's thoughts of Avice the First it is very fully expressed [2] :

" He observed that every aim of those who had brought her up had been to get her away mentally as far as possible from her natural and individual life as an inhabitant of a peculiar island : to make her an exact copy of tens of thousands of other people, in whose circumstances there was nothing special, distinctive, or picturesque ; to teach her to forget all the experiences of her ancestors ; to drown the local ballads by songs purchased at the Budmouth

[1] *The Mayor of Casterbridge*, p. 148.
[2] *The Well-Beloved*, p. 13.

fashionable music-sellers', and the local vocabulary by a governess-tongue of no country at all. She lived in a house that would have been the fortune of an artist, and learnt to draw London suburban villas from printed copies."

The world, then, into which we step when we open the covers of these novels is a world more than ever difficult to find elsewhere in these times of railways, automobiles, mechanical reapers and binders, and trade unions of agricultural workers. Tess, in her print gown and cotton bonnet, watching the gleaming cranks and wheels of the locomotive, is the type of the old world confronting the new. In this Wessex old customs and beliefs have lingered on. The railway is only just stretching out its tentacles into the virgin countryside, and in the more remote districts there live many who have never come into contact with the modern spirit it represents. And since the modern spirit, according to Hardy, is a careworn spirit ; since those best enjoy life who know least about its ways, the simple rustics form the comic relief to his tragedy.

They appear in *Desperate Remedies*, the author's first published work of fiction, and at the end of this novel they act as chorus, effectively describing the wedding of Springrove and Cytherea Graye. Here also an intimate knowledge of rural life is manifested (for example in the place where the passage of a wayfarer through a flock of sheep is marked, some half-an-hour afterwards, by a space in their midst). And

here, in the conversation of Farmer Springrove and
his friend, we find already the note of pagan stoicism
in the face of death. Stoicism, indeed, sometimes
becomes transmuted into something like callous
indifference, though Coggan can find excuses for
Poorgrass, who has dallied at the inn while in
charge of a wagon bearing the coffin of poor Fanny.
" Why should a man put himself in a tearing hurry
for lifeless clay that can neither feel nor see . . . ? "
This complete obliviousness to the claims of proper
reverence and sentiment becomes sheer ghoulishness
when Christopher Coney commits the theft of the
four pennies which have been used to weight the
eyelids of the dead Mrs Henchard. Mrs Cuxsom
is the narrator, and she finishes her account of the
deed by relating :

" ' Faith,' he said, ' why should death rob life o'
fourpence . . . ? '
" ' 'Twas a cannibal deed ! ' deprecated her
listeners.
" ' Gad, then, I won't quite ha'e it,' said Solomon
Longways. ' I say it to-day, and 'tis a Sunday
morning, and I wouldn't speak wrongfully for a
zilver zixpence at such a time. I don't see noo harm
in it. To respect the dead is sound doxology ; and
I wouldn't sell skellintons—leastwise respectable
skellintons—to be varnished for 'natomies, except I
were out of work. But money is scarce, and throats
get dry. Why *should* death rob life o' fourpence ?
I say there was no treason in it.' " [1]

[1] *The Mayor of Casterbridge*, pp. 137-138.

This, with its show of respectability, its qualifications, its Malapropisms and its quaint reasoning, is the grim aspect of the peasant humour (or rather the humorous light in which the author places the peasant), at which we smile, but which outside a work of art would be repulsive.

In *Under the Greenwood Tree* Hardy deals almost exclusively with the villagers, and weaves around them his only wholly idyllic story.[1] Of plot there is little, and the love-making of Dick Dewy and Fancy Day is less interesting than the talking and doing of the Dewy family in general and of the Mellstock Quire. Though no characters occupy prominent positions in more than one novel, as in Balzac, there is bare mention (and occasionally a little more) in some books of personages in others. Among the stalls in Casterbridge Corn-Market at the time of Henchard's residence in that town are those of Everdene (*Far from the Madding Crowd*), Shiner (*Under the Greenwood Tree*) and Darton (*Interlopers at the Knap*), while Everdene and Boldwood appear among the Mayor's creditors. William Dewy is the hero of perhaps the very best of Hardy's humorous tales—that of the praying bull, told by Crick at Talbothays [2]—the family is mentioned in *A Few*

---

[1] H. Child, indeed, denies this (*Thomas Hardy*, 1916, p. 54). He makes much of Fancy Day's temporary disloyalty to Dick, when she accepts Maybold's proposal, only to reject it later. But it is true she keeps this from her husband.

[2] *Tess*, p. 142.

Crusted Characters, and the Quire speak from their graves in the *Wessex Poems*. The men of this famous Mellstock Quire are the embodiment of that love of music which is so noticeable in the Hardy peasant. They play in the west gallery of the church on Sundays, and perform on Christmas Eve for the benefit of residents for miles around. This is their ecclesiastical function, which has gradually been usurped by harmonium and organ—a usurpation which in this place gives rise to a scene of wonderfully rich humour, the visit of protest to the rector,[1] and which is paralleled by the drowning of the boys' voices by those of the schoolgirls below.[2] Their secular function is to play reels and jigs at " randies." Both kinds of music are copied by hand from opposite ends of the same book, and a broadly farcical story (*Absent-Mindedness in a Parish Choir*) deals with the scandal caused by a certain choir striking up *The Devil Among the Tailors* in church, having been suddenly awakened from a sleep induced by the sermon and by imported stimulants.[3] Choirs of this kind have place in other tales among the *Crusted Characters*, in *Two on a Tower* and in *The Mayor of Casterbridge*. They touch, as has been said, the religious and secular life of the people at different times. The religion is that of the Church of England, the metrical versions of the psalms are used, and the carols are simple, graceful and old-fashioned.

[1] *Under the Greenwood Tree*, pp. 79-90.
[2] *Ibid.*, p. 41.   [3] *A Few Crusted Characters*, p. 235.

The rustics are represented for the most part as being under the domination of old superstitions and fetichistic beliefs, over which Christianity has cast only a veneer, but they are well-posted, not only in Biblical lore and language, but also in the detail of the church-service. Lady Constantine's discomposure at the sight of Swithin is marked in the villager's mind by her making the wrong responses ; and the milkmaid Marian, in *Tess*, expresses her shame at walking into church late by colouring up " so hot . . . that I hardly cool down again till we get into the That-it-may-please Thees." They discuss theology in their simple fashion, and refer to the Deity in the most familiar terms, which would seem irreverent if they were not so utterly natural and without consciousness of ill : their reasons, also, for adhering to one denomination rather than another are often in the last degree quaint or frivolous. The landlord in *A Laodicean* ascribes to the local Baptists motives of gain from Paula and the privilege of cheap burial, while his own reasons for becoming a Methodist are, if possible, more ludicrous.[1] Jan Coggan prefers the Church because " a man can belong to the Church and bide in his cheerful old inn, and never trouble or worry his mind about doctrines at all. But to be a meetinger, you must go to chapel in all winds and weathers, and make yerself as frantic as a skit." Mark Clark agrees, however, that " chapel-members " are clever to be able to

[1] *A Laodicean*, pp. 41-42.

"lift up beautiful prayers out of their own heads,"
as Coggan says, whereas "we Churchmen, you see,
must have it all printed beforehand, or, dang it all,
we should no more know what to say to a great
gaffer like the Lord than babes unborn." [1]

Even more powerful than the appeal of the
church-music is that of the profane variety, which
mostly consists of tunes for dancing. Dancing is one
of the chief forms of recreation among Hardy's
peasants, and the dances are of the old country kind,
in the main jigs and reels performed in figures
wherein the couples form a double row and work
up to the top of the set. It takes place in barns,
cleared rooms or in the open air, and any social event
is made an excuse for it. Thus the guests tread a
measure at the Bellstons' christening (in *The Waiting
Supper*), at Dewy's wedding (*Under the Greenwood
Tree*), at Giles's party (*The Woodlanders*), and at
the East Egdon "gipsying" (*The Return of the
Native*). "To dance with a man," says Hardy in one
place, "is to concentrate a twelvemonth's regulation fire upon him in the fragment of an hour";
and on numerous occasions he emphasises the
potency of the dance in arousing emotion, ranging
from the rough revel of the Trantridge folk through
the partnership of Dick and Fancy up to those of
Paula and Somerset and Eustacia and Wildeve.
There is nothing surprising in this emphasis, for
dancing is the response to an impulse as ancient as it

[1] *Far from the Madding Crowd*, p. 328.

82

is widespread, and, in its widely different forms, has been practised by all peoples, from the most savage to the most civilised. The very names of the different tunes have a flavour of bygone times—*Haste to the Wedding*, the *Dashing White Sergeant* and *My Fancy-Lad*. Mop Ollamoor,[1] with his violin, exercises something like a hypnotic power, but he is one of the least convincing figures and properly belongs to the family of *The Pied Piper of Hamelin*. Gabriel Oak is the complete shepherd, not only in his knowledge of the calling, but in that he solaces his lonely hours with melodies on the flute ; and *The Dance at the Phœnix* (in *Wessex Poems*) narrates the story of a middle-aged woman who is irresistibly drawn by the music of a regimental ball to renew the pastime of her youth.

Drinking, of course, occupies a very large place among the activities of the Wessex peasants, and the inn serves as a club where they can forgather. Hardy often pictures them sitting round a room, drinking and giving voice to very profound remarks or retailing local gossip. In *Far from the Madding Crowd* are to be met the members of a circle which forms his greatest triumph in this humorous vein, and best of all scenes is that in Warren's Malthouse,[2] where each personage is sketched in a few words and each remark driven home by a deft explanatory touch. The Malthouse itself is a primitive, stone-

---

[1] *The Fiddler of the Reels* (*Life's Little Ironies*).
[2] *Far from the Madding Crowd*, chap. viii.

flagged place where the ale is brewed on the premises, and it contrasts with the modern, town public-house where Jude's Arabella earns her livelihood for a time. Among these people there is no great talent to distinguish one man from another, and in consequence they pride themselves to a ludicrous extent on some small attainment or on some quality which is outside their control altogether. Thus great amusement is caused by the constable in *The Three Strangers*, whose taste of responsibility turns his head and makes a Dogberry of him ; Corporal Tullidge and Simon Burden, the watchmen in *The Trumpet Major*, speak as though England's safety depended on them. And here, at Warren's, there is much admirable humour in the maltster's pride in his extreme age and that of Joseph Poorgrass in his shyness. Here and in other drinking scenes the gestures, expressions and attitudes of the drinkers and their readiness or otherwise to pay, the degree to which they partake—all these things are conveyed in a vivid manner, which almost makes audible the clinking of the mugs. Rolliver's (in *Tess*) has only an off-licence, and so the parties there are clandestine—a fact which makes necessary a loud-voiced remark from the landlady whenever a step is heard on the stairs : "—Being a few private friends I've asked in to keep up club-walking at my own expense." The peasants possess a fastidious taste in liquor, and this is what leads them to Rolliver's rather than the fully-licensed " Pure Drop" at the other end of the village. Dewy comments on his cider, and knows the kind of apples from which it was pressed—unlike the modern drinker of the town, who only knows that his beverage has come out of a factory. Another method of distinguishing between inns (especially in the country towns) is by their neighbourhood and clientele—witness the three in *The Mayor of Casterbridge* : the "Three Mariners" is a little below the "King's Arms," and lower still is "Peter's Finger" in the disreputable Mixen Lane quarter.

Apart from these more prominent customs of the country, of which the last two (dancing and drinking) survive under different forms and conditions, there are others which have died out altogether, and some of which were peculiar to that part of southern England described by Hardy. The yearly hiring fair is Gabriel Oak's hope of employment, and again gives opportunity for a display of generosity by Farfrae. Other fairs are the sheep fair at Green-hill, where Troy acts Dick Turpin ; the travelling show at Weydon-Priors, where Henchard sells his wife, and another which comes nearest to the modern exemplar in *On the Western Circuit* (*Life's Little Ironies*). At Weydon-Priors the taste for drink is ministered to by the old purveyor of "furmity," a strange concoction of raisins and milk which she surreptitiously "laces" with rum. Hospitality is warm among the rustics : entire choirs practise at Dewys' and Martins', while the shepherd in *The Three Strangers* does not demur (though his wife does) when the traveller makes himself thoroughly at home, and not only drinks deeply of the best ale, but demands tobacco and a pipe. Good-natured heartiness of disposition also makes itself felt in the custom of singing in a body under the windows of a newly married couple. Revels still take place out of doors, as in the East Egdon "gipsying" and the Maypole dancing at Blooms-End (in *The Return of the Native*), and dates in the farmer's year are celebrated; the sheep-shearing on Bathsheba's farm is marked by a supper given to all the hands. Once indeed the arrangement of signalising a public festival by open-air sports (always a matter of anxiety in our climate) is the cause of severe chagrin. When Henchard has caused the erection of greasy poles, the provision of wheelbarrows and donkeys for racing, and all the paraphernalia of a rural jollification, his usual ill-luck pursues him and a rainy day drives the public to the sheltered amusements of his rival, Farfrae.[1] That day, dear even now to the hearts of boys, the 5th of November, is, in *The Return of the Native*,[2] kept up in the orthodox way, with bonfires, but on a larger scale than we find at present; for every hill for miles around is crowned with one, and not only the boys but the

---

[1] *The Mayor of Casterbridge*, p. 120.

[2] Hardy thinks this custom has more to do with "jumbled Druidical rites and Saxon ceremonies" than with the Gunpowder Plot.

older villagers (including the sprightly Grandfer Cantle) assist at the celebration. Clare's first view of Tess is on the occasion of a club-walking, when the women of the Marlott club march two and two round the parish, each bearing a peeled willow wand and a bunch of wild flowers.

The old-world character of this Wessex is the main agency which keeps these peasants so unsophisticated, and it is chiefly preserved by the lack of systematised instruction and the primitive nature of communication which keeps the people out of touch with modern movements and thought. The horse, though still a highly useful animal, is not now, in most places, indispensable, but to the folk of the Wessex Novels he is the life-blood of transport. He it is who pulls the carrier's van of Mrs Dollery or the tranter Dewy, and when Durbeyfield's horse is killed, the haggler's occupation is gone. In the same book occurs the scene of the removal of furniture from house to house, not, as now, in closed pantechnicons, but in farm-carts sent by the new employers of the family or in hired wagons. A world even older than usual is treated in *The Distracted Preacher*, which is a story of smuggling and battles of wit between the excisemen and the dealers in contraband spirits.

Various itinerants perambulate the countryside, testifying to the primitive condition under which goods or services are peddled instead of being drawn from some central source. Quack medical advice is

87

given by Vilbert (in *Jude*), who travels prodigious distances on foot ; and even theology is peddled by a man with a paint-pot, who daubs admonitory texts on gates and blank walls.[1] The grim office of hangman too is not, at that date, performed by one or two professionals who visit the various prisons, but by a local resident whose ordinary occupation is gardening.[2]

The peculiar temperament of the rustics is, of course, evolved partly out of their position as countryfolk in general and partly out of the impact of these various customs and conditions, which are, for the most part, purely local and special. As a body they are ignorant, full of gossip, addicted to drinking and not very strict in morals, but they are kindhearted, frank, generous and slow to take offence. They are specialists in their work, but they do at least learn to follow out their single line efficiently, taking a pride in doing one thing well instead of dissipating their energies in half-doing several things.[3] They are altogether without the pert cocksureness so often found in the lower-class townsman. Social discontent has not yet found its way among them to any great extent, though Marty cannot help contrasting the comfort of Mrs Charmond with her own hard lot, wondering how the fortunate possessor of wealth and position can be bored or ill at ease.

In general the manorial landowners rule over the tenants with unquestioned sway, and there are few signs of any tendency to revolt against inequality. An echo of the older and more cruel times is the introduction of man-traps in *The Woodlanders.* Cruelty in a more subtle form is represented by the "skimmity-ride" or "skimmington," a rough-and-ready method of holding up to derision any couple suspected of a breach of the moral law, by forming a procession headed by a donkey carrying effigies of the offenders. The skimmity-ride which causes the death of Lucetta[1] is engineered by the rough element of Casterbridge, by ne'er-do-wells far removed in character from such people as the Dewys ; for it is to be remarked that, though all the humbler characters have a certain family likeness one to another, each of them has his or her own personality quite clearly defined, and Hardy has more than once protested against the habit of classing all the rural people together and calling them by the collective name of "Hodge." William Worm, though a "wambling man," whose deafness takes the form of head-noises like "frying o' fish," is different from Christian Cantle and Thomas Leaf, half-witted "village idiots," and again from Laban Tall, whose simplicity takes the less serious form of colourless personality, causing him to be known as "Susan Tall's husband." There is the tender, chivalrous, devoted Charley, who so faithfully and

[1] *The Mayor of Casterbridge*, chap. xxxix.

89

CHARACTER AND ENVIRONMENT

vainly loves Eustacia. There is the ridiculously youthful Grandfer Cantle, with his memories of his dashing days with the " Bang-up Locals in 'four." Even the most lightly touched personages are at once singled out by some such phrase as " the wide woman," which clings to Susan Nunsuch. In the last novel of all (*The Well-Beloved*), Hardy draws material from a place more remote and with even stranger and longer unbroken traditions than any of his other settings—the Isle of Slingers, where the inhabitants look upon the mainlanders (" kimberlins ") as foreigners, convey property in church, and carry out old betrothal customs.

It has already been remarked that Hardy represents the peasants as pagans at heart, taking a great interest, it may be, in the external trappings of religion, the church-music and so forth, looking on " pa'sons " as beings of another and more exalted sphere altogether, but unmoved by any deep belief in the Christian theology. Their superstitions, however, are many and varied, and are very seriously believed by all. Witchcraft and " overlooking " on the part of Rhoda Brook [1] are put down as the cause of Gertrude Lodge's diseased arm, and the beautiful Eustacia is believed to be a witch by Susan Nunsuch, who, noticing that her behaviour is somewhat out of the ordinary, comes to the conclusion that she has bewitched the ailing child. She adopts the expedient of stabbing Eustacia's arm with a stocking-

[1] *The Withered Arm* (*Wessex Tales*).

needle, and when this does not remove the malign influence, makes a wax effigy of the supposed enchantress, sticks pins into it and places it in the fire. Even Elfride's dread of Mrs Jethway has in it some lingering elements of superstition which have survived in spite of education. There are fetichistic beliefs too, like Mrs Durbeyfield's dread of sleeping under the same roof as *The Compleat Fortune-Teller* and Tess's chill of fear when she learns that the pillar on which she has sworn is no holy relic, but a memorial to " a malefactor who was tortured there by nailing his hand to a post and afterwards hung." Omens play some part in *Tess of the D'Urbervilles*, and they do in fact turn out to be justified. The churn at Talbothays Dairy one day will produce no butter, which is tentatively explained by Mrs Crick as the result of somebody's being in love, and in fact, as the reader knows, two persons *are* in love. Then on the wedding-day of Tess and Clare a cock crows thrice in the afternoon—an evil omen only too well fulfilled.

One story in *A Few Crusted Characters*, told by the Superstitious Man, relates how an apparition of William Privett appeared in a place connected with his life at the very moment when he was passing away. There is excellent fun connected with an omen in the conversation between Fairway and Christian Cantle, when the former gravely sympathises with Christian on being born when the moon was new :

" ' Mother know'd 'twas no moon, for she asked another woman that had an almanac, as she did whenever a boy was born to her, because of the saying, "No moon, no man," which made her afeard every man-child she had. Do ye really think it serious, Mister Fairway, that there was no moon ? '

" ' Yes ; " No moon, no man." 'Tis one of the truest sayings ever spit out. The boy never comes to anything that's born at new moon. A bad job for thee, Christian, that you should have showed your nose then of all days in the month.'

" ' I suppose the moon was terrible full when you were born ? ' said Christian, with a look of hopeless admiration at Fairway.

" 'Well, 'a was not new,' Mr Fairway replied, with a disinterested gaze." [1]

A minute later Fairway deepens the depression of the shuddering Christian by assuring him that he is likely to be the recipient of a visit from a ghost, since he can persuade no woman to marry him, and ghosts never appear to married people. Prognostication is attempted half-humorously in Bathsheba's manipulation of Bible and key. It is believed in by Henchard (who has a strong superstitious strain) so implicitly that he regulates his commercial dealings on the basis of Conjuror Fall's weather-forecast, with disastrous results. These "Conjurors" are the object of a secret respect on the part of the natives of Wessex, who, pretending to discredit them, yet shamefacedly seek their advice. Conjuror Trendle

[1] *The Return of the Native*, p. 28.

is consulted by Mrs Lodge, and it is he who, after performing mysterious rites with a glass of water and the white of an egg, informs her that the only cure for her withered arm is to touch with it the neck of a man newly hanged. Both these conjurors are mentioned by name at Talbothays on the occasion of the trouble with the butter.

Another form taken by superstition is the belief in the efficacy of some act quite irrelevant to the situation in averting or lessening evil. Of this nature are the ringing of the bells backward at the " Three Tranters " fire in *Desperate Remedies* [1] and the singing of the Talbothays dairy-hands to secure a better flow of milk from the cows, which have secreted it in their horns because of the coming of a new worker ! [2] Discussion of this leads to Crick's story before mentioned, wherein William Dewy escapes from a ferocious bull by playing the Nativity Hymn—a proceeding which brings the pious animal to its knees. [3] A similar belief concerns bees : all the hives are tapped to awaken their inhabitants when a death occurs, lest all the bees should die too. [4]

Two other forms remain to be mentioned, and both are more widely known than the others— namely, love charms or forecasts and historic apparitions. The former is exemplified in the philtre of the quack Vilbert, [5] and the visit to the woods of the

[1] P. 196.   [2] *Tess*, p. 141.   [3] *Ibid.*, pp. 142-143.
[4] *Interlopers at the Knap (Wessex Tales).*   [5] *Jude*, p. 491.

Hintock girls on Old Midsummer's Eve,[1] with the object of finding out whom they are destined to marry. The latter includes the D'Urberville Coach and the vision of Hadrian's soldiery seen by old folks in the Ring at Casterbridge.

These, then, are some of the customs and superstitions of Hardy's Wessex. They are closely interwoven with the life of the people, and would, in themselves, make the subject of a fascinating study. Without them the peasants of these novels would not be the same, and their presence once again shows not only that Hardy wished to enshrine such temporary but beautiful things in his art, but also that in their interaction with rustic character, he has in mind, as always, that " inevitableness of character and environment in working out destiny " of which he writes elsewhere.[2]

[1] *The Woodlanders*, chap. xx.
[2] *The Profitable Reading of Fiction* (*The Forum*, March 1888).

CHAPTER IV

THROUGH many of the Wessex Novels and tales
runs an historical undercurrent which affects the
reader's idea of the life set forth therein and frequently makes itself felt in the working out of the
characters as a determining factor in their predilec-
tions. Side by side with the close view of mankind
as a community made up of widely differing indi-
viduals is the broad, sweeping view which takes in
humanity as a part (if the most important part) of
the world, and each personage as a part of the race.
In various places the unchanged character of a
district throughout the centuries is indicated by the
presence of prehistoric barrows and tumuli, just as
the persistence of pre-Christian fetichism is more
than hinted at in descriptions of peasant folk-lore,
customs and temperament. The chapters dealing
with Egdon Heath in *The Return of the Native*
gain much in effect through this practice : Domes-
day and Leland are cited, their words on the subject proving that the Heath was much the same in
those historic times ; while Eustacia makes her first

95

appearance standing on Rainbarrow, a mound rising in the loneliest part of this waste. Later, in the days of her sorrow and estrangement from Clym, the devoted Charley endeavours to please and distract her by bringing in curious objects, including " stone arrow-heads used by the old tribes on Egdon ": a very boyish consolation, albeit simple and kindly. By a number of minor references such as these the immense antiquity of Egdon, its untamable nature, its grim character, are brought home to a reader with such effect as to make quite plausible the strong influence it exerts on the minds of the various characters.

The story, *A Tryst at an Ancient Earthwork*,[1] has no plot at all. It is simply an account of an antiquarian's visit to the ancient stronghold of Mai-Dun and the result of his excavations there ; but it is told with a wealth of imaginative detail which makes it as effective as many a story of excitement and action. The darkness of the night, the surreptitious character of the visit, the impressiveness of the fortress, and above all its associations with living men of fifteen hundred years ago (driven home, finally, by the discovery of a skeleton of a warrior who had fallen in battle)—these things combine to produce a tale of great interest and beauty.

The Mayor of Casterbridge, of which the scene is laid principally in Casterbridge (Dorchester), gives more fully than any of the other novels a description

[1] *A Changed Man and Other Tales*, 1913.

96

of a town; in this instance an old-world town. Henchard is a man of old-fashioned methods, and it is noticeable that until the advent of the innovating Farfrae these methods are not considered a disadvantage. The spirit of the place is quiet and sleepy; its life is bound up with the past. It is still (in the times of which Hardy writes) stamped with a semi-Roman character, and under its soil, easily discovered by digging, lie the skeletons of Roman soldiers. The Amphitheatre, on its outskirts, has a melancholy reputation. Old folk possessing vivid imaginations have reported visions of Hadrian's soldiery seen there, and the place is never used for lovers' appointments or any meetings of a cheerful nature.

Hardy has never written an historical romance, pure and simple, but his interest in historical tradition is always strong, and *The Trumpet Major* is placed in the times when the people of southern England were living in continual apprehension of an invasion by Napoleon's army. This novel is partly founded on stories told to Hardy in his youth by old people who could remember the days of the Napoleonic wars. The interest created in his mind by the researches necessary to the writing of *The Trumpet Major* led to a deeper general interest in the period, which ultimately bore fruit in the great epic-drama of *The Dynasts*.[1] Several short stories (as, for example, *The Melancholy Hussar of the German Legion*, one of the *Wessex Tales*) relate to

[1] *Vide* Preface to *The Dynasts*.

97

the same historical time, and others (like *Master John Horseleigh, Knight* [1]) go back further into the past. One whole series, *A Group of Noble Dames*, is entirely devoted to an imaginative elaboration of happenings of which the bare details have been gleaned from old pedigrees, pipe-rolls and the like. Studies in local folk-lore and tradition very naturally go along with studies in genealogy and local history, so it is not surprising to find that Hardy is interested in the latter as well as in the former. There can be no question but that his estimate of men is made on the basis of moral character alone, disregarding ancestry and exalted rank ; but, among the minor beauties of our English life, this very English writer includes " the boast of heraldry, the pomp of power," and quite naturally and inevitably reckons a sense of lineage among the less weighty factors which go to make up the temperaments of some of his personages, and in one case (that of Paula Power and the de Stancys) gives it considerable importance.

In respect of this influence a short story may be taken as the text and essence of the whole series. Squire Petrick's wife (the sixth " Noble Dame "), on her deathbed, tells her husband that the son he had supposed to be his, really owns as father the Marquis of Christminster. After cutting young Rupert out of the entail, in his first chagrin, Petrick gradually comes to feel pride in the supposed noble parentage of the boy, and, by forging the date on

[1] *A Changed Man*, etc.

an old will, reinstates him in the succession. But Rupert resembles Petrick, and a doctor tells the Squire that Annetta's "confession" was probably the delusion of an hysterical woman. Petrick ends by despising his own son as a mere commoner. This tale, then, displays in its most extreme form the reverence for blue blood working on the mind of a man who, one would think, has every reason to feel bitter against the aristocrat until the true state of affairs comes to light. It will be observed that the point of interest lies in psychology rather than in outward action. This is true of all Hardy's work, even in the historical sphere, wherein most writers concentrate on action. *Barbara of the House of Grebe*,[1] in fact, is a somewhat ghastly narration, and is as modern as *Jude the Obscure* or *The Withered Arm* in its recognition of the interplay of psychological and pathological forces.

The earliest instance of a strong interest in genealogy is provided by the Rev. Mr Swancourt, father of Elfride, in *A Pair of Blue Eyes*. He is a Tory of the Tories, full of respect for the aristocracy and its accomplishments: he takes a liking for young Smith, and, though puzzled at his pronunciation of Latin and his inability to ride, takes pains to persuade himself that Stephen belongs to an old family of Smiths once eminent in the neighbourhood. The humour of this is evident, not only because of the architect's real parentage, but because of his

[1] *A Group of Noble Dames* (Dame 2).

name, the most common of all purely English surnames. Next in time comes Sergeant Troy, who
commands considerable respect on account of his
position as the offshoot of a noble family. With him
may be grouped Fitzpiers, whose forbears at one
time owned the Manor and lands around Oakbury
Fitzpiers. Both these men retain some of the outward polish derived from their connection with the
polite world, but both have become depraved in respect of true worth, and are contrasted unfavourably,
the one with Oak and the other with Winterborne.
Lord Mountclere (in *The Hand of Ethelberta*) is
a still more depraved scion of an old stock. He
is a thoroughly debauched and evil old reprobate :
his vices are the more nauseous because they are not
merely the failings of a young man, and he lacks the
redeeming traits which blunt the condemnation of
Fitzpiers. In him Hardy gives the extreme instance
of a man noble only in name and not in nature.

A very striking fact concerning *Tess of the
D'Urbervilles* is that every aspect of Hardy's art and
thought is therein exemplified. The main interest
of the story, of course, lies in the heroine's encounter
with convention ; but whether the critic be in search
of pathos, humour, irony, tragedy, description of
nature, superstitions or folk-lore, some striking
example will at once arise in his mind from this
book. Except in architectonic quality (wherein it
is inferior to *The Return of the Native*) it is the
greatest of all the novels. The historical interest,

though not paramount, gives the title to *Tess*, and
is intimately bound up with the theme. Tess is " of
the D'Urbervilles," an ancient and knightly family,
descended from a Norman knight, and once the
owners of wide estates in Wessex. The revelation
of this family history by Parson Tringham is the immediate cause of John Durbeyfield's foolish, boast-
ful behaviour and the proximate cause of Tess's visit
to "The Slopes." That the quondam owners of
the soil should now be among the workers employed
thereon is by no means a unique state of affairs ;
Retty Priddle comes of the once powerful Paridelles,
and there are others among the peasants likewise of
old lineage. As with Elfride and Viviette, Tess's
courage fails her when she attempts to enlighten
Clare as to her past life, and she substitutes a lesser
confession for a greater, telling him that she is a
D'Urberville. He makes light of it at the time,
but afterwards brings it up against her :

" ' I cannot help associating your decline as a
family with this other fact—of your want of firmness.
Decrepit families imply decrepit wills, decrepit conduct. Heaven, why did you give me a handle for
despising you more by informing me of your descent!
Here was I thinking you a new-sprung child of
nature ; there were you, the belated seedling of an
effete aristocracy!' " [1]

Clare is interested in old families in the same way
that an agnostic might be interested in church-music

[1] *Tess*, p. 297.

or a humanitarian in hunting. There is nothing inconsistent in thus admiring the artistic side of a thing while strongly disapproving of it on purely rational grounds. In conversation with his father, Clare thus expresses his feelings in the matter :

" Politically I am sceptical as to the virtue of their being old . . . but lyrically, dramatically, and even historically, I am tenderly attached to them." [1]

One of the distinguishing characteristics of romanticism in English literature is a deep appreciation of the mediæval age of chivalry. Bishop Hurd, in the middle of the eighteenth century, associated his plea for romantic subjects [2] with a defence of this age, and in the work of Sir Walter Scott the historical interest became paramount. Paula Power, in *A Laodicean*, presents the spectacle of the two forces of classicism and romanticism struggling for ascendancy in a modern mind. Paula's personality, as the author himself confesses in the preface, is elusive and difficult to sum up, as are the traits which make her beautiful. Her intellectual life is passed in contact with the forces just named, and her emotional life exhibits a conflict between impulsiveness and a more than Scotch caution, which for a considerable time prevents her from burning her boats behind her. The strength of her neo-Grecian leanings may be gauged by her persistency in the design of having an incongruous Greek court built

[1] *Tess*, p. 213.　　　　[2] *Letters on Chivalry and Romance.*

in the Gothic Stancy Castle. Her capitulation on this point comes just when Somerset has decided, against his better judgment, to give in to her whim —a *volte-face* typical of Hardy's women. Paula at first takes little interest in the historical appurtenances of the Castle, and Charlotte de Stancy (herself a member of the ancient family who once owned it) takes even less. The influence of the historic past plays about both of them, effecting in Charlotte no reaction, and in Paula, at the outset, a negative one, alienating rather than arousing her sympathies. Of this tendency the Grecian tastes show one aspect and the desire to make the most of the modern conveniences of life shows another. Paula has nothing in her of the *parvenue*. How absolutely free she is from any shade of patronage or vulgar pride in her wealth is made evident by the strong bond of friendship between her and Charlotte, who, in her position of the dispossessed, would have found the least touch of these things intolerable. But Paula is clever, self-reliant and modern in her ideas. She has no thought of using her wealth for the acquisition of a factitious nobility, but she is quite determined to spare no expense in making the Castle habitable and comfortable. It seems clear that Hardy intends the telegraph to stand as a symbol of modernism impinging on mediævalism; for when Somerset first follows the wire, it leads him to Stancy Castle, and this intensely modern thing enters through an arrow-slit from which Tudor archers were wont to launch their missiles at the foe. Hardy gives us, in Paula, a girl dowered with beauty, intelligence and wealth, of a reserved and somewhat dispassionate nature, developing her character under the three influences of religion, mediævalism and love. At the time of our introduction to her the religious influence is definitely on the wane. She has never been temperamentally drawn towards the tenets of the strict Baptists, and it is only at the desire of her late father that she has continued outwardly to conform. From the time of her revulsion against baptism the gap between her and Woodwell's community becomes wider, and a factor helping to widen it is the second of the influences mentioned —mediævalism—which is in the ascendant, and which draws her towards the picturesque and " Gothic " in contradistinction to the atmosphere of plain simplicity in which the Baptists move. There remains the conflict between love on the one hand, and mediævalism and a sluggish emotional nature on the other, in which love eventually becomes the victor. Paula's tantalising attitude towards Somerset is not due merely to the desire to give no excuse for the wagging of village tongues ; it has a deeper root in her constitutional inability to give herself up completely to any impulse or pursuit, and it is from this characteristic that the book takes its title. With the advent of de Stancy, mediævalism gains considerable ground, especially when Somerset is slandered through the machinations of Dare.

IN THE NOVELS OF THOMAS HARDY

Paula, even after she has at last made up her mind and acted, is last heard of on a note of vacillation—" I wish my castle wasn't burnt ; and I wish you were a de Stancy ! " are her last words to Somerset.

CHAPTER V

INTELLECTUAL AND ARTISTIC INFLUENCES

It is trite but true to say that any psychology which professed to account entirely for a given personality by studying in detail the intellectual influences which had been brought to bear on it would be doomed to failure and error at the outset, for it would be dealing, at best, with only half the forces which serve to mould human character. Two girls are brought up together in a convent : one becomes a nun, the other an actress. Cases like this are common, everyday experience, and serve to show that the innate basis of a character is the crucial factor which determines its reaction to its environment, and that any estimate which is attempted must necessarily be incomplete if it does not take into account emotional and other complications. Throughout this study this point of view is assumed, and it is not to be supposed that Hardy is represented as accounting for the conduct of Tess *solely* by convention or that of Troy *solely* by occupation. None the less we do usually find that one set of influences is predominant in directing the courses of the lives which he treats.

106

Intellectual preoccupations are quite outside the ken of the "stoic heroes," Winterborne, Oak and Venn, and of that of those women who are closest to the soil, like Marty, Thomasin and Tess. But in the mental make-up of the more highly educated people they naturally take a prominent place. Knight and Clare have certain affinities, but they differ from Jude, Yeobright, Pierston and Fitzpiers, while each of these, in his turn, again differs from the others. Likewise Sue is very unlike Elfride, and Ethelberta is very unlike Grace, who bears a certain general resemblance to Yeobright. Yet Grace and Ethelberta have both been subjected to an almost identical transmutation. Ethelberta, lifted out of a simple, rustic family, clings to her new advantages at all costs—even at the cost of marrying a man she does not love. Grace, similarly taken out of her old *milieu*, is only superficially touched by the changed circumstances, and very soon manifests the desire to slip back into the ways to which she was born. These men and women are the *intelligentsia* of the Wessex Novels. To say this is not, of course, to say that they are the only "intellectuals" of the series. There are others who clearly come under the denomination, such as Lucetta, Mrs Charmond, Neigh, Bathsheba, Paula and St Cleeve, but they are either minor characters, or else they seem to fall more naturally into other divisions.

It is in his third novel, *A Pair of Blue Eyes*, that Hardy first shows clear signs of the point of view which afterwards becomes so prominent in his studies of character. Even in *Desperate Remedies* there are traits similar to those of his later work (thus early, " when," as he ironically says, in his preface of 1895, " there was no French name for them "); but it is only in the later book that there emerges the clear conception of characters working out their destiny not only under the sway of external influences but also in accord with a predisposing mental bias, which may or may not be increased by outward events. Such characters are Elfride and Knight. Since Mr Swancourt is a widower, Elfride is the apple of his eye. She, being a young lady of some skill with the pen, often writes his sermons for him. Not content with these minor literary efforts, she writes an historical romance, which is accepted and published, but rather severely reviewed in one of the journals by a reviewer who afterwards becomes known to her as Henry Knight. Elfride's situation is that of a very alert mind coupled with strong and wayward emotions coming into contact with a much stronger mind in which emotion has been dulled and hardened by an almost monastic devotion to intellectual pursuits. The opening sentence of the book relates that her " emotions lay very near the surface." She is, by reason of her isolated existence, unpractised in the ways of the world, so that when she falls in love with the young Stephen Smith she does not understand that the love of eighteen seldom has elements of permanence and

108

pins her faith in its continuance, thus causing untold anxiety to herself later on, and the utmost misery to the unfortunate Smith. Of course no lover of eighteen has any qualms on the insecurity of his or her affections (which are all the nobler and purer for this blissful ignorance), but few take the extreme step that Elfride takes. The flight to London is a rash and romantic proceeding, and when Elfride's vacillation at the last moment causes her to return unmarried, she meets the one person in the world who has a motive (real or fancied) to besmirch her reputation—Mrs Jethway. This is only one of the many coincidences on which the plot of *A Pair of Blue Eyes* rests over-heavily ; other notable ones, on which much hangs, are that Knight happens to be a connection of the second Mrs Swancourt, and that it is he who is chosen to review Elfride's book.

Elfride is the type *par excellence* of Hardy's view of the educated woman. Education has superimposed a great deal, but has left untouched the fundamental attributes of the sex. She is intellectual without being a bluestocking, but the forces which direct her actions in moments of stress are not those of reason but of primitive emotion. Her personality is radiant and charming, with a charm all the greater by virtue of her freshness and inexperience. But Hardy conveys in a subtle and convincing manner the idea that in matters of the affections there is no safety in presupposing consistent and honourable conduct on the part of a woman, be she never so inexperienced and seemingly ingenuous. There is no need to saddle Hardy with the extreme and absurdly one-sided views of Schopenhauer in this matter; it is simply a fresh and very skilful working-out of an ancient and widespread conception. Nevertheless in one respect Schopenhauer seems reasonable—when, in the famous *Essay*, he attributes this unexpected subtlety in the apparently ingenuous woman to the fact that for countless ages woman has had but one profession. Elfride's deceit, when it comes, is anything but deliberate. It is deep-seated and instinctive—so much so that she even deceives herself until the cliff-rescue brings full consciousness that Knight and not Smith is the loved one. She acts despicably towards Smith, particularly in the Luxellian vault, where she accepts his noble (if quixotic) attitude of a mere acquaintance, yet in spite of all, and against all reason, she is a lovable character.

Coming within the orbit of Knight, she proves her complete womanhood by falling a victim to his superior powers, in this case mental. Smith makes the mistake of being too uniformly kind, whereas Knight unwittingly takes the more efficacious way of domination, without at first being actuated by any ulterior motives. There is much irony in the situation of the three. Smith, looking up to Knight as the noblest man in the land, and his own particular benefactor, who has helped him in many ways by advice and teaching, praises him so highly

that Elfride is jealous, putting to Stephen the old
casuistical problem, Which of the two would he save
from drowning if he were only able to save one?
Yet in a few months the eternal paradox has been
illustrated in the gradual attraction of Elfride by a
personality towards which her first feelings have been
antagonistic. The two games of chess may serve as
pointers to the state of affairs between Elfride and
the two men. When she plays against Smith she is
superior and endeavours to let him win, but in the
game with Knight it is he who is the more expert,
and who at first tries to follow this patronising procedure. In spite of her vivaciousness and superficial
frothiness, it is plain that Elfride is a thinking woman.
If nothing more were taken into account, it is no
small accomplishment in a girl of nineteen to write
a novel of a high enough quality to find a publisher ;
but apart from this, she is able to talk intelligently
to Knight, and she has flashes of insight which are
beyond the capacity of Smith, as he himself recognises :

" 'Stephen, I fancy I see the difference between
me and you—between men and women generally,
perhaps. I am content to build happiness on any
accidental basis that may lie near at hand ; you are
for making a world to suit your happiness.'
" 'Elfride, you sometimes say things which make
you seem suddenly to become five years older than
you are, or than I am ; and that remark is one. I
couldn't think so *old* as that, try how I might.' " [1]

[1] *A Pair of Blue Eyes*, p. 64.

Such speeches in Elfride's mouth are not rare, and they show her as above the average girl of her age in the power of generalising and expressing her ideas. It is through a sense of pique and intellectual rivalry that her feeling for Knight develops. He is at no pains to conceal his contempt for her understanding, her love of finery, and her tomboy pranks (like that of risking her life on the parapet of the church-tower). He refuses to compliment her by saying that his taste is for brown hair and blue eyes when he rather prefers dark hair and hazel eyes. And so the battle goes on between them, ending in the complete capitulation of Elfride. True to his type, Knight is somewhat lukewarm in his love-making, but this only serves as an additional attraction to Elfride, whose affection reaches such a pitch of intensity that it is not damped but fanned by his priggish desertion. From the story told by Unity at the end of the book, it is clear that her second love is not only strong but enduring, and that her marriage with Lord Luxellian is only a *pis aller*, Knight's image being firmly fixed in her mind to the end. Pity is kindled for Elfride, especially when she impulsively seeks Knight out at his London apartment, careless of pride, reputation and anything but her love. The person most deserving of pity, however, is the frank, chivalrous and straightforward Smith, who bears himself throughout with honour and even an excess of humility, both in respect of his claims on Elfride and on Knight. If there be some measure of poetic justice in her sorrow and in Knight's, this cannot be said of Smith, whose only faults have been extravagant trust and modesty.

In all the highly developed intellectual men of Hardy's novels there is some trait or combination of traits which repels. This fact, of course, is the corollary of the aforementioned presentment of the simple rustic character as the acme of nobility and dignity. It is a curious thought that men of high intellectual power sometimes take great pains to portray men of similar power as lacking in warmth or in principle ; in the same way that we find anti-rationalists constantly exhausting all the resources of their own reason in the effort to decry reason! Wordsworth extends his praise of the rustic even to his language, making out a very plausible contention, until the answer comes from Coleridge in terms of hard common sense. What Coleridge sees, and what neither Wordsworth nor Hardy sees, is that the artist unconsciously projects his *own* thoughts and feelings into the breasts of the uncultured people he describes; that a very large proportion of country-dwellers are quite insensible to the beauty which surrounds them :

" Education, or original sensibility, or both, must pre-exist, if the changes, forms, and incidents of nature are to prove a sufficient stimulant. And where these are not sufficient, the mind contracts and hardens by want of stimulants, and the man becomes selfish, sensual, gross, and hard-hearted." [1]

[1] *Biographia Literaria*, p. 164 (Bell, 1894).

At the same time it may be granted that in respect of isolated cases there is an element of truth in Hardy's apotheosis of the peasant and disparagement of the cultivated man, though it would be unsound to base a generalisation thereon. Leaving aside the general question, and considering the particular embodiments of this feeling, they will be found to vary in their degrees of verisimilitude. It is hard to believe that any man could have been so stiff-necked and hard-hearted as Clare or Knight. On the other hand, Yeobright is quite natural; he has the complete wrong-headedness and unpracticalness of the true doctrinaire. Fitzpiers is excellently delineated (he is one of the most skilfully drawn characters in the whole series), and Jude likewise. Pierston, though the underlying idea is true, is somewhat exaggerated in respect of his chronic fickleness.

The intellectual and artistic influences which have been brought to bear on Henry Knight are, in the main, those of literature. He has travelled in Europe, it is true, but evidently with his eyes only half-open. He has had a classical education at Oxford (or perhaps one should say " Christminster ") which, while it has laid the foundations of a sound literary taste, has also left behind it something less worthy. There is something intolerable in his patronising attitude towards Stephen Smith. Here is an account of the younger man's reception by the elder :

"Knight did not rise. He looked at a timepiece on the mantelshelf, then turned again to his letters, pointing to a chair.

"'Well, I am glad you have come. I only returned to town yesterday ; now, don't speak, Stephen, for ten minutes ; I have just that time to the late post. At the eleventh minute, I'm your man!'" [1]

Worse even than this is Knight's conduct in the Luxellian vault, though Hardy does not seem to represent him there intentionally in a very unfavourable light. He is unaware that Stephen knows Elfride ; much less does he suspect that she is the fiancée of whom the young architect has spoken. He does not even introduce Elfride, because " Smith was still the country lad whom he had patronized and tended ; one to whom the formal presentation of a lady betrothed to himself would have seemed incongruous and absurd." [2] Those who have met men of this stamp will feel that they could well have spared the pleasure. Knight's attainments, though not spurious, have unfortunately made him both a social and an intellectual snob ; and his extravagant requirements from the woman he chooses show him to be a prig. Still, it is true that he himself offers the same thing that he requires, whereas Angel Clare, meeting with a real breach of the moral law in his beloved, has himself been guilty of a similar breach.

There are men who can study literature for years without applying their knowledge to life itself.

[1] *A Pair of Blue Eyes*, p. 143.   [2] *Ibid.*, p. 295.

They approach books as one might approach numismatics or conchology, and never seem to realise that an attitude of complete detachment towards literature, an attitude which takes the thoughts of authors as things to be tried by some esoteric rule and not by their relation to actual life, is productive of crabbedness and sterility. Such a man is Henry Knight, who, on the verge of middle-age, expects to mate with absolute inexperience, and rejects a true and strong affection because his lady has had a childish love-affair. He has that " unhealthy virtue " of which Maeterlinck writes, saying that " toute vertu est maladive à laquelle nous attachons une grande importance et pour laquelle nous exigeons une attention respectueuse." [1] Knight attaches too much importance to his own untouched affections, the condition of which may be due not to superior virtue but to a hardening of the mind and an innate coldness of temperament. He demonstrates the truth of another of Maeterlinck's words of wisdom :

" Dans l'amour comme dans la vie, il est presque toujours fort inutile d'attendre; c'est en aimant qu'on apprend à aimer, et c'est avec les soi-disant désillusions des petites [sic] amours, qu'on nourrira le plus simplement et le plus sûrement la flamme inébranlable du grand amour qui viendra peut-être éclairer le reste de la vie." [2]

Angel Clare is a man of wider culture than Knight, and his conduct towards Tess is as severe

[1] *La Sagesse et la Destinée*, chap. cx. [2] *Ibid.*, chap. cxii.

as that of the reviewer towards Elfride and even
more surprising. Educated with a view to the
University, to be followed by ordination, he shows
at last that he is not cast in the same mould as
his conventional brothers, who pursue the path of
respectability and become most respectable curates.
Angel acquires the habit of thinking for himself,
and finds that he is unable to compromise with a
system which seems to him founded on a false
philosophy. An agnostic in religious matters, he
begins to feel that if the traditional faith has turned
out hollow in one sphere, it may be so in another ;
thus " he began to evince considerable indifference
to social forms and observances. The material
distinctions of rank and wealth he increasingly despised." Somewhat strangely, his agnosticism seems
to have originated in admiration for the old pagan
times, not from the usual source of such a point
of view—a sense of the incompatibility between
the ancient Jewish mythology and modern scientific
thought. None the less, the process going on in his
mind during the years of transition is a rationalistic
one ; he still respects traditions, but comes to believe that they can survive only if they are supported
by some greater thing than the sentiment cling-
ing to them through their age. The rationalist
who has been brought up in an atmosphere
impregnated with the old faith must inevitably
feel some loss on the emotional side to counter-
balance the intellectual gain which results from the

117

casting off of the fetters of dogma. He will most probably then turn to art and nature as outlets for the energy which he formerly expended in religious devotion. Clare does this, taking sustenance for his imagination in the classic stories, in the beauty of the country where he learns his trade, in music, and finally in his love for Tess. His love for her is peculiar in its quality, spiritual and yet warm, not aroused by beauty or character alone, but also by a kind of worship of a type. She is to him the embodiment of country freshness, innocence and grace, she is " brim full of poetry—actualized poetry." He might have said of her :

> " She seemed a thing that could not feel
> The touch of earthly years."

It is as this type, the " virginal daughter of Nature," that he woos and wins her. It is not surprising that Tess's confession comes as a shattering blow, that Clare is prostrated with the terrible grief of his disillusionment. The extraordinary thing is that he is so obstinately tenacious of his point in the face of the humble and pathetic half-hopefulness with which Tess awaits his forgiveness. He remains obdurate in circumstances which seem warranted to melt a heart of stone. Where now is his freethought ? Where now his unconventionality ? Early training shows up through the veneer of later emancipation which his character has taken on, and, knowing all the details of her story, knowing that she has freely forgiven him for the identical fault, he insists that the woman he has been loving is not she but another in her shape. In truth he has been loving an idea, an abstraction, not a woman, and when he finds that the living, breathing, human being no longer corresponds to the abstraction, he will not be content to forgive and accept a rare wealth of devotion. He must go. It is patent that his subconscious self is warring against the decree of the conscious idealist : the fine scene of his sleep-walking proves this. But in the cold light of day his reason approves of the course he has decided on, and when he relents it is too late. True it is that he has more to forgive than has Knight ; but it is also true that he cannot bring forward any plea of continence on his own side. He seems to attach very little importance to his own moral lapse, complacently accepting different codes of conduct for men and women. Well as he knows Tess, he seems unable to see (once the confession is made) that all her instincts are pure, and that it is far more through misfortune than through viciousness that she has fallen into sin. It is a strange trait in human nature that the " ethereal " lover can be absolutely harsh and callous once he perceives some falling-away from his ideal, or when he himself has deserted it. The Clare who proposes an elopement to Izz Huett is only less inconsistent and cruel than the author of *Epipsychidion*, who writes to propose that his lawful wife shall join him and his mistress in their

Continental home. Such inconsistency between principle and practice, such illogicality of the logician, round off and consummate the tragedy of Tess.

The factor which produces the final rupture between Clym Yeobright and Eustacia Vye is intrinsically a much smaller thing than those which cause the respective breaches in the cases of Knight and Elfride and Clare and Tess. In its essence the mere refusal to answer a knock at the door is a very slight matter, but (as often in Hardy and in life) it has great and terrible consequences. The very beginning of Clym's love-affair is inauspicious. He has been sent away from Egdon at an early age, placed in trade, and has finally won a solid position for himself materially. His worldly success, however, leaves a spiritual void in Clym's mind. He has the philosophic temperament, with a special bias towards social reform, which becomes in time a passion : he is seized with the desire to give up working for his personal advantage and to work for the uplifting of his fellow-men. So far, so good : we are impelled to admire the nobility of his self-sacrifice. But when the actual putting into practice of the idea comes to the forefront, the situation becomes greatly complicated ; a whole host of personal and other considerations enter into it, as they must enter into any such project. Firstly, there is the question (which does not occur to Clym, though it certainly does to his creator) of how far what we call education is conducive to happiness (for it is in the sphere of education that Clym decides to work). Secondly, there is the question whether enlightenment or social amelioration should come first. The first question brings up one of the great paradoxes of life. It is certain that education increases man's capacity for joy and his opportunity to do good, but it is equally certain that it augments his capacity for pain and his opportunity to do evil. The initial description of Clym at the beginning of Book 3 voices clearly the view that increase of knowledge brings disillusionment and sorrow : it is one of Hardy's grievances against the Architect of this world that the desire for knowledge has been implanted in the breasts of the better part of mankind, while its gratification brings care, worry and neurosis in its train ; whereas those who are insensible to the call of intellect and live nearer to the animal plane are often more healthy in body and more quiet in mind. Clym is an instance of this. Had he never left the Heath, never come into contact with the wider life of the world, he might have been tolerably contented. But fate willed it that he should spend his days in a great metropolis, disgusted with his trade in " the especial symbols of self-indulgence and vainglory," until at last he returns to his native place, hoping to lose his *malaise* in a new life of self-effacement and effort. His ill-luck brings him to semi-blindness, effectually preventing the fulfilment of his plans ; but even had this physical disability not supervened, we are left with a doubt as to whether he would have brought peace to his own soul or enlightenment to his countrymen. "We can hardly imagine," Hardy writes, "bucolic placidity quickening to intellectual aims without imagining social aims as the transitional phase." Again, "In consequence of this relatively advanced position, Yeobright might have been called unfortunate. The rural world was not ripe for him." Not only the rural world, but the whole world of modern society, permeated as it is by commercialism, is still unripe for such as he ; and a further paradox is that an artistic temperament can be a very expensive thing in the upkeep, while, generally speaking, the temperament and the means of its indulgence seldom go together.

Unfortunately for himself and all connected with him, Clym is unable to see the greater good he might have done by working for himself antecedently to or concurrently with his work for mankind. He is unable to compromise with a world that delights in diamonds and draw sustenance from a state of affairs while at the same time trying to reform it. There is something great in the serenity with which he follows his fixed purpose and bears his misfortune, but there is also something chilly and adamantine. The great man, according to Carlyle, must be consumed by an inward fire. The question is whether he is justified in overriding all personal ties and claims if they stand in the way of his idea. Rightly or wrongly, Mrs Yeobright objects to the schoolmaster scheme and to Eustacia ; rightly or wrongly Eustacia objects to the schoolmaster scheme and to Egdon. Here is a maze of conflicting aspirations indeed! Clym's method is to press on in his own course ; and though we must admire the single-mindedness of his devotion to an ideal, we must recognise that it bears with it a considerable amount of that egoism which is always found in the doctrinaire. " Nothing," says Burke, in the *Letter to a Noble Lord*, " can be conceived more hard than the heart of a thoroughbred metaphysician " (meaning a doctrinaire political philosopher).

Mrs Yeobright's behaviour is enough to exasper-ate a saint, but Clym's perversity is more strongly shown in his treatment of Eustacia than in that of his mother. He marries Eustacia with his eyes wide open ; he knows that she will never be content to remain in a hut on Egdon ; he even makes certain definite promises. Then he does not attempt to understand Eustacia or to meet her half-way in any of her wishes ; he does not stop to inquire into the real circumstances of the shutting-out of Mrs Yeobright (which are vastly less damaging to Eustacia than he supposes), but assails his wife with coarse abuse. After her departure he shows his monstrous egoism still further by writing in this strain : " Why have you not come before ? Do you think I will not listen to you? Surely not, when you remember the kisses and vows we exchanged under the summer moon." There is something almost nauseating in this kind of appeal from one who wishes to " be pardoned and retain the offence." As an abstract idealist Clym stands high, but as a man, in his dealings with the persons who stand nearest to him, he is like Knight and Clare in leaving much to be desired.

One of the most curious psychological problems presented to the reader of Thomas Hardy is the character of Edred Fitzpiers, and the would-be interpreter must walk warily when he comes to consider Hardy's own attitude towards this erring physician. The preface to *The Woodlanders* bears more than a touch of irony in the sentence : ". . . it is tacitly assumed for the purpose of the story that no doubt of the depravity of the erratic heart who feels some third person to be better suited to his or her tastes than the one with whom he has contracted to live, enters the head of reader or writer for a moment." But does the ironical reference apply to Grace's second thoughts about Winterborne alone, or does it contain also an allusion to Fitzpiers's renewed passion for Mrs Charmond ? There can be not the slightest doubt but that the feeling between Grace and Giles is on a much higher plane than that between Fitzpiers and Felice, but the fact remains that in both cases a mistake is felt to have been made. It is undoubtedly true that Fitzpiers is of a sensual nature, lacking in restraint and moral fibre, where Winterborne has both in abundance : nevertheless, if one thing is certain in the novel it is the beauty of Grace's character, and in the end, when Fitzpiers has gone through the fires of remorse and served a long probation, she returns to him under no coercion but that of her own feelings. Mr John Freeman [1] thinks Fitzpiers and Mrs Charmond "failures in portraiture," and is of opinion that the return of Grace to her husband is "one of many stealthy stabs at the persistence of the common view of marriage." Hardy, we may be sure, would disclaim the intention of "stabbing" at anything. What he does, in this book, and with still more emphasis in *Jude the Obscure*, is to show by the interplay of a number of varying characters that marriage is often contracted under the influence of a passion quite temporary in character, and that no mere repetition of responses, no legal or sacerdotal sanction, can make it a marriage in anything but name, in the absence of deeper and more permanent feelings between the persons concerned.

It has been seen how various intellectual influences exercise a hardening effect on the minds of such men as Knight, Clare and Yeobright, leading them to expect more from human nature than it can give, and bringing about tragedy by preserving in them an unbending attitude when one small concession of sympathy might have saved all. Similar influences work in quite a different way upon the personality of Fitzpiers, because his besetting sin is not over-coldness of temperament but, on the

[1] *The Moderns*, Thomas Hardy, 1916.

contrary, an undue warmth. He is more of a dilettante in his learning than the other three : anatomy, chemistry, metaphysics, poetry are some of the subjects which occupy his fertile but wayward mind in the Hintock solitudes. But he is conscious of the limitations of his sphere and frets under them. Made for society and clever circles, he is here without outlet for his energies, and he seethes and bubbles with repressed activity, mental and emotional. His fatal weakness is that he cannot wait and be sure of himself, and so he falls into grossness and marital infidelity. There is no palliation for the intrigue with Suke, nor indeed for that with Felice, but the latter can be shown to be very natural in view of the peculiar circumstances. To his sentimental heart Felice is a memory of a two-days' youthful passion at Heidelberg. She is a finished coquette, a cultivated woman, a woman of family, and she can play on every key of this mind which responds so readily to a new sensation. To crown all, her affection is forbidden fruit. Given Fitzpiers's temperament and the circumstances named, it is inevitable that he shall succumb. At the end of the book he appears in a new and better light, but there is no inconsistency in this.

Apart from his one great failing, he has never been wholly despicable, and the experiences he goes through serve to tame the wayward side of his nature and bring him back to decency through the valley of humiliation. One matter, indeed, Hardy

seems to have managed clumsily. This is the shoot-
ing of Felice by her melodramatic foreign lover, who
plays an insignificant part otherwise in the action of
the novel. It is too convenient and opportune, but
this or something similar had to be engineered if
Fitzpiers was to return to Grace and prove his
penitence. At the last he shows that his culture is
by no means altogether an artificial thing, thinly
covering his animal nature. It has required a terrible
shock and a feeling of loss to drive into the depths of
his nature the realisation of the really worthy things
of life, to bring home to him that the admirable
purity and beauty of Grace's nature are beyond all
computation more worthy to be followed than the
satisfactions of sordid intrigue. But once that realisation has been driven home he is a changed man. His
conduct at the deathbed of Giles and many other
things show extreme delicacy of feeling. His self-
abasement and repentance are complete, and they are
amply rewarded. The tragedy of the book lies not
so much in the temporary sorrows of Grace, as in the
death of Winterborne and the bereavement of Marty,
for these two were naturally fitted for one another.

The root cause of all the emotional troubles
in *The Woodlanders* is Melbury's ambition to raise
his daughter out of the social sphere in which she
was born, by means of education. Like Yeobright,
Grace is transplanted from her native Wessex and
made to pursue a totally different course of life ; and
she also is a " native " who " returns " to the scenes

of her childhood and tends to fall back into the old ways of thought and conduct. At first, however, this throwing off of the new is a slow process. It is at once apparent that where Grace has moved on, Giles has stood still (though in Hardy's view he is none the worse for this). He lacks some of the qualities which would make him a fit partner for Grace, and it is Grace's misfortune that the only man possessing those qualities who comes within her orbit is lamentably deficient in the more important direction—that of moral character. Grace's emotional attitude after Winterborne's death is somewhat of a puzzle. Her devotion to his memory is complete at the outset, and it is only by long and gentle persuasion, clenched by the incident of the man-trap, that Fitzpiers succeeds in finding his way back into her affections. We may perhaps imagine the couple, both sadder and wiser, reaching a true understanding at length, but it seems inevitable that there should remain one corner of Grace's heart into which Fitzpiers can never penetrate, for it is occupied by the memory of one whose devotion was such that he gave up life itself rather than risk a breath of scandal on his lady's name.

The transplantation spoken of above, the entire removal of a personage from one environment to another of a very different nature, seems to have held out great attractions to Hardy. Two more examples thereof may be taken in Ethelberta Petherwin and Jocelyn Pierston.

Ethelberta stands apart from Yeobright, Pierston and Grace Melbury in that the change in her circumstances is on the whole to her advantage. It is true that she crowns her career by marrying an objectionable old titled libertine, but in the last glimpse of her we see that she has taken him in hand and reformed him so far as may be, and her aspirations have always been material ones. So Ethelberta, according to her lights, wins success. She is the least attractive of the gallery of women portrayed in the Wessex Novels. In her we see little of the charm and fascination of an Elfride, none of the gentle appeal of a Tess. Nearer to her than any of the others are Paula and Bathsheba, but both these betray weaknesses which make them more lovable. From the point of view of policy, Ethelberta never makes a mistake. She is flinty-hearty, and unworthy of the faithful Christopher Julian, who meets a better reward in the hand of the delightful Picotee. The one aspect of her personality we can admire is her extreme thoroughness. Gifted with a fine brain, she knows that the social position to which she has climbed is her true one, and she is determined to keep it at almost any cost. When Neigh is pressing his suit, she is less concerned with the emotional aspect of the situation than with the material side ; her eminently practical proceeding of going down to investigate his property at Farnfield is a pointer to her character. Other illuminating facts with reference to Ethelberta are her attitude towards her family, her method of earning a living, and, above all, her search for sanctions for her projected marriage in a work on utilitarianism. Nevertheless her worldly ambition is by no means wholly selfish. She has that hardness possessed by all Hardy's highly intellectual personages, but she is genuinely solicitous for her family's welfare, and all her working and scheming is as much for them as for herself. Her creator is very lenient with her. His apology takes the usual line— that man is the creature of circumstance : " She had begun as a poet of the Satanic school in a sweetened form ; she was ending as a pseudo-utilitarian. Was there ever such a transmutation effected before by the action of a hard environment ? " [1]

The general level of characterisation in *The Hand of Ethelberta* is poor when compared with that in the novels dealing more particularly with the country people of Wessex. In this " Comedy in chapters " there are a great many people who indulge in very clever conversation, and the author imports their pseudo-cleverness into his own style. The resultant reads like a parody of Wilde or Meredith : it is not Hardy's *forte* ; it is not convincing, and, with the exception of *Desperate Remedies* and *The Well-Beloved*, this book is of less account than any in the series.

The Well-Beloved is avowedly a fantasy. Jocelyn Pierston, a son of the Isle of Slingers, " the home

[1] *The Hand of Ethelberta*, pp. 320-321.

of a curious and well-nigh distinct people, cherishing strange beliefs and singular customs," becomes a famous sculptor and a man of fashion, but never altogether loses the dreamy temperament developed by his early life on the island. On his first return to the home of his people his shock of surprise on being greeted in the old, free manner by Avice Caro is the first indication of the sophisticating process wrought in him by change of scene and occupation. The plot of the book is absurd, but allowing for the exaggeration permissible in a work of this nature, Pierston's character does exemplify a side of human nature overmuch neglected by novelists. The man who marries his first love is, in real life, the exception, whereas in novels he is the rule. Most men do, in fact, cherish the image of their Well-Beloved, which dwells first in one woman and then another, but few carry fickleness to the extreme length to which Pierston carries it. It is notable that the only women in whom the Well-Beloved abides for long are women from his native place. When at last rejected by the third Avice, it is to Marcia (who has played Capulet to his Montague forty years before) that Pierston returns. There is rather a ghastly irony in this mating, and it is accentuated by the total loss of artistic taste and genius which befalls the sculptor after his illness, and by the utilitarian enterprises in the Isle of Slingers (once the home of his dreams), which are his last recorded acts.

131

CHARACTER AND ENVIRONMENT

From the intellectual point of view, Sue Bride-head is by far the most highly developed woman in Hardy's pages. At first glance it might appear that she was of intellect "all compact," heartless and lacking in generous feeling. But the matter is not so simple : if this were all, she would have aroused no passion, particularly in a man of Jude's tempera-ment, and she would not be surrounded with the atmosphere of fascination which does in fact float about her in the earlier parts of her appearance in the story. Sue has gone further in free-thought than even Angel Clare. Her rationalism, like his, originates in admiration for pagan thought and in-stitutions rather than in a feeling that science and philosophy have sapped the foundations of the old faith ; but she is much more iconoclastic than he in her dealings with tradition. The model of Jerusalem, displayed for the edification of the school-children, cannot hold her interest for long : from her stand-point, her words on the subject are perfectly just and logical, however disconcerting to the orthodox : "There was nothing first-rate about the place, or people, after all—as there was about Athens, Rome, Alexandria, and other old cities." [1] Christminster, to her, is "a place full of fetichists and ghost-seers" [2]; she is impatient of its mediævalism be-cause she has reached the stage of thought which recognises that a beautiful thing (*pace* Keats) is not necessarily true in the objective sense, and that

[1] *Jude*, p. 125. [2] *Ibid.*, p. 181.

132

underneath outward peace and grandeur may exist a world of prejudice, injustice and narrowness. Jude, finding her employed as an ecclesiastical designer, expects her to be imbued with the Christminster spirit ; instead of which she proves to be out of sympathy with the place, with her occupation and with the beliefs which it subserves. This distaste extends even to Gothic architecture, and the immediate cause of her dismissal from Miss Fontover's shop is a quarrel over two statuettes of Venus and Apollo which Sue has bought.

All these are questions such as agitated more masculine than feminine minds in those days ; but Sue has been no ordinary girl. She has lived a life of exceptional freedom for a woman at that date, reading where she listed and mixing with men as a friend and equal without any sentimental complications ensuing on her side. Her " curious unconsciousness of gender " is indeed the salient point in her character. She is quite sensible of it herself ; it leads to situations trying, delicate, and even disastrous; it is the more tantalising to Jude in that it breaks down at times and erects a barrier on other occasions when he least expects it. One day she writes a friendly or even affectionate note, signed " Sue "; the next day comes a cousinly letter in the opposite mood, marked by the signature " Susanna Florence Mary Bridehead." Her alternations of passion and discretion are bewildering : she can play with Jude as a cat with a mouse ; if he is annoyed

133

at her inconsistency she charms his anger away, only to repulse him again a few moments later. It is never made clear why she marries Phillotson. When she contracts this alliance she knows of no bar to her union with Jude, yet she continues with the project which, in view of her later feelings towards her husband, she must know to be an insane one. She is undoubtedly highly strung and nervous, but to sneer " Neurotic! " even, does not account for all. Intellectually and in theory she is mistress of herself and knows what she ought to do ; but when faced with an emotional problem, she cannot gauge her own feelings from one minute to the next. She is swayed by every wind that blows— affection for Jude, jealousy of Arabella, repulsion for Phillotson ; and her retrogression after the loss of her children, urged by a perverted sense of duty, goes beyond the pathetic into the horrible. This lovely, bright-souled, ethereal creature, half woman and half spirit, is a masterly study in abnormal psychology : she is a study for the psycho-analyst ; and the play of intellectual influences on a personality such as hers presents problems which will become more frequent and urgent as time goes on and civilisation becomes more complicated.

The short story, *An Imaginative Woman* (which first appeared in *Wessex Tales* and was afterwards transferred to a more appropriate place among *Life's Little Ironies*), presents Hardy's philosophy of the action of environment on character in its most striking and concentrated form. He here deals again with an abnormal woman, but he carefully points out in the preface that the extraordinary manifestation on which the story turns is " well supported by the experiences of medical men." Ella Marchmill is " an impressionable, palpitating creature," yoked in marriage to a matter-of-fact gunmaker, without refinement or imagination, though usually kind. With him Ella's artistic and emotional nature is starved ; she takes refuge in a world of her own, a world of poetry and fancy. Placed by chance in the very room of her long-admired poet, Trewe, living among his books, reading his poems and seeing even the scribblings which it has been his habit to make on the wallpaper above the bed, she becomes enamoured of a personality similar to her own, but much stronger and more finely endowed. Her suburban life of comparative loneliness is conducive to introspection, and her commonplace environment seems to press more closely on her after the experience at Solentsea. More and more her feelings fasten on the image of the adored but unmet Trewe, so that the bitter disappointment when his proposed visit is abandoned, followed by the shock of his suicide, serve to hasten on her own death. The statement in his last letter, that he is destroying himself largely because he despairs of ever finding a person in tune with him, is the crowning irony, and the whole experience is strong enough to leave its physical impress on Ella's child.

CHAPTER VI

CONVENTION : SOCIAL, THEOLOGICAL AND MORAL

The lives of all civilised men are affected by a set of laws other than those comprised in the code of their native country; laws possessing more elasticity, perhaps, than the written ones, but less easy to keep faithfully and often very severe in the infliction of penalties, by reason of the frequent capriciousness of their operation. The idea of property, the collective realisation of *meum* and *tuum*, is the foundation-stone of the social life of any peaceful and orderly community, and hence we find more regular laws dealing directly or indirectly with this matter than with any other. Without security of property, either privately or collectively owned, no civilised state could exist. Other affairs equally or more important to the individual have been found less so to the commonweal, and have therefore been left more to the regulation of those unwritten laws which we call the conventions. Conventions possess varying degrees of importance, from the cut of a coat to that of a creed, and they change from year to year and between nation and nation. No man can afford to neglect them altogether, yet no man could possibly

136

follow them always in their entirety. Those who affect to despise the familiar conventions completely only succeed in setting up a fresh code of less rational ones : an amusing essay could be written on " The Conventionality of the Unconventional," satirising the practices of the *soi-disant* " Bohemians." No less ridiculous are those who worship at the shrine of Propriety with excessive devotion, losing a great deal of the harmless joy arising out of human frailty. Since the conventions are so many and varied, it follows naturally enough that some are more worthy of support than others. All have originally had some good reason behind them, for they have not been imposed by any *fiat* of a supreme authority, but have grown up out of the collective common sense of a people. They are given the status of a goddess in Samuel Butler's *Erewhon*, in a chapter full of brilliant insight into the subject.[1] Her name is Ydgrun, and Butler sums her up as follows :

" Take her all in all, however, she was a beneficent and useful deity, who did not care how much she was denied so long as she was obeyed and feared, and who kept hundreds of thousands in those paths which make life tolerably happy, who would never have been kept there otherwise, and over whom a higher and more spiritual ideal would have had no power." [2]

[1] Chap. xvii., *Ydgrun and the Ydgrunites*. ("Ydgrun," of course, = " Grundy.")

[2] *Erewhon*, p. 175 (Fifield, 1917).

137

The point at which a convention becomes mischievous and dangerous is when it has outlived the necessity which gave rise to it, or when a situation arises which cannot properly be dealt with by the application of rough-and-ready general principles.

Every bold pioneer of thought is put down by the crowd as unconventional, for he brings a message that the day of the old outlook is done. Then the heresy of to-day becomes the orthodoxy of to-morrow, and the process is repeated by later thinkers *ad infinitum*. This holds good of Thomas Hardy. His work is full of challenge to orthodox beliefs, particularly on the moral and theological sides, and in *Tess* and *Jude* his indignation against some aspects of orthodoxy burns at white-heat. Even in the thirty-odd years which have passed since these works appeared, public opinion has greatly advanced, and it is difficult to-day to realise the tremendous audacity of the standpoint there taken up unless we plunge into the controversial literature to which the said novels gave rise.[1]

Hardy has obviously been struck by the great, and in his view disproportionate, part played by the goddess Ydgrun in determining the courses and ultimate fate of man. He has, in *Tess* and *Jude*,

---

[1] See, *e.g.*, T. G. Selby, *Theology of Modern Fiction*, 1896, chapter on Hardy. In the magazine version of *Tess*, D'Urberville arranges a "fake" marriage. Such were the concessions exacted by Victorian respectability! (*Vide* Beach, *The Technique of Thomas Hardy*, p. 201.)

used this factor as the mainspring of great works of art, and constantly throughout the other books and the poems he exposes the artificiality which comes about when convention is *slavishly* followed for its own sake and not for any inherent rationality at its root.

Unlike the younger Wells, Shaw and Galsworthy, Hardy keeps his political opinions strictly in the background. In this, posterity will probably acclaim his wisdom, for political interest is the most ephemeral of things, and nothing is so wearisome as old-fashioned politics. Such a novel as *Ann Veronica* and such a play as *John Bull's Other Island*, for example, are already hopelessly "dated." They rely mainly on issues which are now dead, whereas Hardy has chosen always to depend for his main interest on the eternal clash of human aspirations and passions, one with another and all with fate. This being so, the social conventions are but lightly touched upon (such things as class-distinctions, that is to say). We have already seen in Chapter III. that the rustics in general accept the current social divisions with small thought of the possibility of any other, and small desire for any change. In *The Hand of Ethelberta*, indeed, there is a much more strongly marked sense of these inequalities than elsewhere. Sol Chickerel seems to be a socialist in embryo ; some of Ethelberta's least laudable characteristics come out in her attempts to evade the discovery of her origin ; and when that origin is at last laid bare by her father, the effect on Neigh and the Doncasters is that of a thunderbolt. But the whole presentation of the " Society " personages is too obviously one-sided. In scenes such as that wherein the assembled company listens to the singing of Ethelberta's song, an incredible insincerity is ascribed to all the auditors. Perhaps the most telling stroke of satire is that the prosperity of Neigh, the man-about-town, should be based on a knacker's ugly yard ; but it is the graphic description of Ethelberta's nocturnal visit to Farnfield which impresses most, and to call the man " Neigh " is rather too crude! Slighter strokes at modern English superficiality are present also. The state of mind which is afraid of being thought capable of the appreciation of deep matters is a very common one in our Island. Such a mind is Mrs Belmaine's :

" ' Milton, thou shouldst be living at this hour : England hath need of thee—'

said Mrs Belmaine with the degree of flippancy which is considered correct for immortal verse, the Bible, God, etc., in these days." [1]

Wherever there is question of theology, Hardy brings out well the significance of the enormous web of convention with which the subject is involved. To him the metaphysic and the historical bases of Christianity are unacceptable, while its ethic, though beautiful, is inadequate and more honoured

[1] P. 211.

in the breach than the observance even by its professed teachers. In his view there is no necessary connection between theology and morals : the fulfilment of rites, the observance of forms may leave a man unchanged so far as moral character goes, and an undue insistence on rites, forms and stereotyped judgments may pervert character by inducing hypocrisy. How this may come about appears in Tess's encounter with the Vicar after the death of her baby. His natural, kindly feelings prompt him to assure Tess that her irregular baptism of the child will suffice to bring its soul to salvation ; but when she comes to the question of a Christian burial, he is (to use Hardy's own word) " cornered," and is compelled to refuse. Again she makes a heart-broken appeal for counsel on the baby's prospects in the life to come : " Will it be just the same ? "

" How the Vicar reconciled his answer with the strict notions he supposed himself to hold on these subjects it is beyond a layman's power to tell, though not to excuse. Somewhat moved, he said in this case also—

" ' It will be just the same.' " [1]

Tess is continually coming into conflict with theological conventions, which serve to increase her confusion and sense of injustice. The phenomenon of the man who defaces the countryside by painting red texts on gates and blank walls draws from Hardy the reflection : " Alas, poor Theology ! " and from

[1] *Tess*, p. 122.

Tess the words : " Pooh—I don't believe God said such things!"

The Clare household and their friend Mercy Chant present several aspects of religiosity. Parson Clare, the father, is eloquent, forceful and sincere. To his own view of life, narrow though it be, he is unflinchingly faithful, counting all work and knowledge useless which is not devoted to what he calls "the glory of God." His uprightness, sincerity and readiness to forgive insult claim the reader's respect, in spite of his inability to see the use of a Cambridge training unless as a stepping-stone to ordination, and his horror when he hears the communion-table called the "altar." But a small incident shows how even a kind heart may, under compulsion of excessive altruistic zeal, display a certain obtuseness to the claims of personal sentiment. Charles Lamb, in the *Essay on Roast Pig*, records how, in his early youth, he was given a cake by his aunt ; how he presented it to an importunate beggar, and how his conscience afterwards upbraided him for this slight to the generosity of the donor, who had, after all, made the present to *him* and no other. Just such an action is that of the Clares, who give Mrs Crick's black-puddings to the family of a man afflicted with delirium tremens, and deposit her mead in the medicine-closet as too strong for ordinary consumption.[1] Still, even the heterodox Angel has nothing

---

[1] *Tess*, p. 207. That the man's disease should be delirium tremens is, of course, a characteristic piece of Hardy's irony.

142

but admiration for the unworldliness and courage of his father. It is when this genuine religious zeal becomes degraded into mere formalism and conscious respectability, as it does in the minds of Felix and Cuthbert, that it arouses Hardy's contempt.

These two young gentlemen belong to a familiar type, long derided in farce and light comedy, but still to be found in many a suburban drawing-room:

> "They were both somewhat short-sighted, and when it was the custom to wear a single eyeglass and string they wore a single eyeglass and string; when it was the custom to wear a double glass they wore a double glass; when it was the custom to wear spectacles they wore spectacles straightway, all without reference to the particular variety of defect in their own vision. When Wordsworth was enthroned they carried pocket copies; and when Shelley was belittled they allowed him to grow dusty on their shelves. . . ."[1]

Mercy Chant is only lightly sketched, as are Felix and Cuthbert, but the portrait is skilfully done. Around every church there gathers a circle of Mercy Chants, assiduous in the performance of "parish-work," meticulous in the following of ritual, hanging on every word of the clergyman, as though he were a superman. Self-righteous, carping, full of acerbity towards the more humane sides of life, they follow the practices of religion and observe all its conventions without inquiring whether there are

[1] *Tess*, p. 204.

not many fine and noble things outside that narrow circle. The few words Miss Chant speaks are thoroughly in character. For example, when one of the Clares suggests that the pair of boots found in the hedge (having been left there by Tess) may have been thrown away by some tramp, she is ready to put the worst construction on the matter by suspecting that the supposed tramp is " Some impostor who wished to come into the town barefoot, perhaps, and so excite our sympathies."

Bishop Helmsdale, in *Two on a Tower*, displays a similar uncharitableness and readiness to look for the worst motive in his encounter with Swithin St Cleeve. This Bishop is a minor masterpiece in everything he says and does. He is not without good sense and sound ideas, as his remarks on the relationship between genius and objective achievements show, but he is soaked in ecclesiastical conventionalism, and his efforts to preserve the dignity of his position while pursuing his courtship of Viviette are very amusing. Hardy has studied the psychology of the cleric very closely, for even the most minute strokes of description show keen insight. On Viviette's unexpected absence from the table, the Bishop sits down, " endeavouring to mould into the form of episcopal serenity an expression which was really one of common human disappointment." His letter containing the proposal of marriage evinces a great deal of candour and common sense, but it is marred by the writer's too profound sense of his own importance and the eminence of his position. For one action of Viviette's there can be no justification—her marriage with the Bishop under the compulsion of circumstances : he has no grave defect of character, and nothing can make this cruel deception excusable.

Stockdale, in *The Distracted Preacher (Wessex Tales)*, is another cleric whose natural, human feelings are at war with the conventionalism imposed on him by his profession. This fine story, full of action and humour, brings out in striking fashion the struggle between Stockdale's respectability and his love for the pretty, adventurous, forceful Lizzy Newberry, who embroils him in several smuggling escapades, and will not give up her nefarious practices in order to marry him. It is only when the contraband trade is crushed by the excise officers and Lizzy's occupation is gone that she consents to become a minister's wife. Respectability triumphs, it is true, but the metamorphosis of the fair smuggler into the tract-writing lady of the manse leaves a feeling of loss to romance. A note to the collected edition of 1912 explains that this ending was made to suit the taste of the magazine-public of the day.

The ambitions of Jude, though he does not at first perceive it himself, are more worldly than spiritual. Even in the early stages of his pursuit of learning he is struck by the incongruity between the pagan mythology which forms such a large part of the subject-matter of his reading and the sacred profession which he proposes to adopt. Thoughts of becoming a bishop or an archdeacon are entwined with his desire to enter the Church, showing once again Hardy's contention that conformity to tradition has no necessary connection with high moral purpose. Another matter which he makes clear in this book, and in *Tess of the D'Urbervilles*, is that some processes which at first sight seem spiritual are in fact psychological : that changes which may seem to come about through the operation of the judgment are, in fact, frequently to be explained in terms of pathology. Such is the dreadful " conversion " of Sue, which leads her to offer herself up as a human sacrifice on the altar of Propriety. After her assertion of freedom, after Jude's emancipation under her guidance, comes the ghastly tragedy, which, through the shock to her overwrought nervous system, drives her back to a submissiveness that is half insane. There are many sad and moving passages in Hardy, but Sue's rejection of Jude and free-thought and return to Phillotson and conformity almost overstep the bounds of tragic art. The implication is still more clear in the case of Alec D'Urberville, where a whole paragraph is devoted to showing how all those features and characteristics which formerly indicated worship of Venus are, by a sudden emotional shock, turned temporarily to quite another worship. Even Arabella, having lost Cartlett, turns to chapel-going until she hears news of Jude.[1] Mercy Chant's mysticism is not similarly accounted for by Hardy, but this is probably because she is a minor figure, not because he did not perceive the repression which causes the overflow of energy, in such cases, through other channels.

As the whole essence of the belief in the power of intellectual influences is concentrated in *An Imaginative Woman*, so is the church influence brought out in another fine story, *A Tragedy of Two Ambitions* (*Life's Little Ironies*). The ambitions of Joshua and Cornelius Halborough are entirely social and worldly : they enter the Church primarily to obtain money and social prestige, and the Gospel which they are to preach is only a means to those ends. Cornelius is the more human of the two. He at least makes no pretence of disinterested motives, and it is he who unhesitatingly runs forward to rescue the drunken millwright from the weir, only to be plucked back by the restraining arm of his more cold-blooded brother. Joshua writes in a letter : " To succeed in the Church, people must believe in you, first of all as a gentleman, secondly as a man of means, thirdly as a scholar, fourthly as a preacher, fifthly, perhaps,

---

[1] *Jude*, p. 377 : " ' After Cartlett's death I was passing the chapel in the street next ours, and I went into it for shelter from a shower of rain. I felt a need of some sort of support under my loss, and, as 'twas righter than gin, I took to going there regular, and found it a great comfort.' "

as a Christian. . . ." The only good quality in these characters is their solicitude for their sister's welfare, but even this is grossly material, and we might well imagine them casting her off altogether if she had not wished to marry Fullmer. Tortured by conscience, harrowed by reading the burial service over their own father as "the Body of an Adult Male Person Unknown," mocked by the flourishing sapling that was once his walking-stick, balked even in their place-hunting, life does indeed vent its irony on these unhappy brothers. The greatest ironies of all are that the worthless father excites no jot of sympathy, and that the hard work and efforts of the Halboroughs would have been in some degree praiseworthy had they not hypocritically chosen to direct their endeavours into a channel which should be reserved for more idealistic and altruistic aspirations.

Two parsons in the series are very unsuccessful in subduing their natural *joie-de-vivre* into the true clerical mould. Swancourt, in *A Pair of Blue Eyes*, is simply a country squire in broadcloth; his temperament has taken on only the thinnest veneer from his profession. Toogood, in *Andrey Satchel and the Parson* (*A Few Crusted Characters*), lives for his hunting, and a very humorous account is given of his ride to hounds, oblivious of the couple locked up in the church tower awaiting his performance of the marriage ceremony.

In all Hardy's presentments of the clergy, in all

his dealings with matters theological, the point of view he takes up is that the really important things are not dogmas,[1] but honesty, justice, generosity, unselfishness and steadfastness under " the slings and arrows of outrageous fortune." Any convention which leads to the opposite of these is harmful, no matter how much weight may be laid upon it by influential cults. When Christian theology attempts to stand in the way of enlightenment, he is against it. In so far as it produces men like the young Clares and the Halboroughs, he is against it. He is far from " denying the beauty and faithful service of certain venerable cults," but at the same time he refuses to disallow the " obstinate questionings " which virile minds are impelled to make, relative to the government of the universe.[2] His only hope for the Churches is that they shall apply " the principle of evolution to their own faith," [2] and he thinks that the English Church is the most inclined to do this. He has lived to see a profound change in the clerical attitude towards Darwinism at least, since Huxley fought with Gladstone and Dr Wace. Recent Anglican and even Romanist pronouncements have shown a tendency towards endeavouring to square the beliefs of these Churches with the discoveries of science.

[1] Vide *Jude*, p. 407. In the moment of their agony, Jude and Sue hear " two clergymen of different views, arguing about the eastward position." The irony is obvious and bitter.

[2] Preface, *Late Lyrics and Earlier*, 1922.

149

CHARACTER AND ENVIRONMENT

Hardy is the possessor of an intensely practical mind, a mind which cannot harbour any trace of cant or obscurantism. Mr Scott-James [1] well says of him that his test for a theory is : " Does the key fit ? " If it does not, then it is the wrong key, and no argument, no weight of assertion to the contrary can make it anything else. This test is brought into play above all in the two great convention-novels which come near the end of the series. The title page of *Tess of the D'Urbervilles* gives out a challenge. This girl, who has committed an action which, from the strict conventional points of view of morals and religion, puts her outside the pale of respectability, is put forward as " a pure woman, faithfully presented." There was a great deal more audacity in thus defining her in 1891 than there would be now, for public opinion has gradually become more liberal in matters of this nature. There is a growing tendency to demand equal standards of morality for men and women, and an increasing feeling that motherhood, lawful or unlawful, is sacred and should be so recognised, if this can be done without encouraging laxity and making wholesale havoc among very necessary and salutary social laws. But Hardy does not set out with the intention of asking *forgiveness* for Tess, and, as it were, smuggling her up the back-stairs to some heaven of the coldly virtuous. He is bolder than Hawthorne, and roundly implies that there is here nothing to forgive. There is a

[1] In *Modernism and Romance*, chap. v., 1908.

clash between social and natural law—or natural indifference and lawlessness. The great "Nescience,"
which has made us what we are, has implanted deep
in our being certain needs which are the strongest
powers within us, and at the same time ironically
ordained that a stable society is only possible when
they are continually repressed. When they escape
repression, society wreaks a terrible vengeance on
one of the transgressors—the woman (to whom
Nature herself seems unfair), who, in this instance,
bears far less guilt than the man. Hardy knows well
enough the wrongs done by women to men, as he
shows in *A Pair of Blue Eyes, Far from the Madding
Crowd, The Return of the Native* and *Jude the
Obscure*.[1] But "nature's holy plan" (which he
quotes, while asking for the poet's authority for the
adjective) has ordained that the wrongs done by men
to women should bring a still more crushing afflic-
tion to her, who *may* be the weaker vessel and *may*
be led astray. The "may" must be emphasised,
for in *Jude the Obscure* Hardy presents the converse
case, wherein a coarse woman is the seducer of a man
of fine potentialities, and ruins him as completely
as D'Urberville ruins Tess. In either event, he implies, the fault lies less in the poor human puppets
than in a dispensation which throws discordant
elements into juxtaposition.

We have already seen (in Chapter I.) how Tess's

[1] It should be said that J. W. Cunliffe points this out
(*English Literature during the Last Half-century*, 1908).

upbringing and home environment operate to bring about her disaster. The whole circumstances of her initial lapse are such as to absolve her from blame, for D'Urberville uses every art and subterfuge ; and not only does she not encourage him, but puts up a spirited defence. Her surrender is of short duration and is succeeded by an immediate feeling of remorse and of dislike for D'Urberville. Any consideration of expediency, any ignoble attempt to make capital out of her situation, by agitating for marriage or accepting presents, are outside the realm of her thought altogether : such ideas do not even occur to her, and her first thought is to go away from Trantridge to a place where she is never likely to see D'Urberville again. How far her morality is above that of such village girls as Arabella (to take an extreme case), or even Izz, Marian and Retty, is brought out by the story of Jack Dollop and his inamorata. This story, which the dairy people treat as a rare joke, jars severely on the more delicate and refined nature of Tess, who sees that, in spite of its ludicrous setting, it has the same elements of tragedy as her own, particularly when seen from the point of view of the principal actor. The frog in the fable said to his tormentors : " What is sport to you is death to me," and what was sport to the milkers was social death to the girl in question. As the history unfolds itself it becomes abundantly clear that, given his premises and neglecting the " artificial and derivative meaning "

of the " sub-title adjective," [1] Hardy has established
beyond question the innate purity of Tess's motives,
which,

> " Fair as a star, when only one
> Is shining in the sky,"

stand out the more brilliantly in contrast with
the various degrees of darkness in the surrounding
characters. Contrast her with Mercy Chant in the
same book ; or go back a hundred and fifty years and
contrast her with Pamela, that virtuous young lady
who was too " canny " to fall into irregular practice
but had no objection to her would-be seducer when
he offered marriage and a coach. Pamela commits
many sins from which Tess is free. Pursued as Tess
is pursued, her surrender is not the result of natural
impulse, but the culmination of a strategical move :
she desires to marry Mr B. and marries him, when
dignity and morality would have driven her to leave
his household at the earliest opportunity. Now from
all this kind of manœuvring Tess is " worlds away,"
and all her dealings with Clare go to show her trans-
parent honesty and strong moral sense, which drives
her into a very ferment of self-condemnation.

All the resources of Hardy's art are lavished
on the picture of this " almost standard woman ":
she stands apart from the others in having nothing
of the coquette in her composition. The reason
for this is probably that Tess is to be shown as a

[1] Preface, 1891.

thoroughly genuine woman who is cruelly punished both by nature and society for a lapse committed in extenuating circumstances. How different might have been the outcome if Clare had been sufficiently large-minded to see that the Tess of his adoration was in very truth the real Tess, notwithstanding the fact newly brought to his notice! The enormous power of the ruling convention, however, makes itself felt in Clare's mind when his vaunted emancipation has to confront a personal issue. But deeper still goes the implication. Tess has committed no sin in the eyes of Nature; yet the social law must be upheld, or civilisation would fall and chaos supervene. Why do social law and natural law contradict one another? Hardy would say that it is not the novelist's business to answer that question. He can only show in his work that the opposition exists and brings about tragedy.

In the story of Jude Fawley there is even closer questioning of current conventions and moral theories than in that of Tess, for there are palliations of Tess's guilt which might be recognised even by a moderately advanced thinker; whereas for Jude there can be no extenuation unless the judge be as far advanced as Hardy himself. Jude, like Tess, is the sport of destiny, but, unlike her, he goes out of his way to seek temptation. Perhaps his most despicable action is that which so distresses the more refined nature of Sue—namely, his renewal of relations with Arabella after her return from Australia (quite

154

legally, of course, but not morally). The animal part of him is always too strong for the spiritual, but if that were all, *Jude the Obscure* would be no more than a record of one of the seamy sides of life, and it is much more than that. Jude has three battles to fight—a social struggle, an intellectual struggle, and a moral struggle. All are more or less interdependent. The moral struggle begins with Arabella's coarse message, characteristically and ironically at the very moment when Jude is taking stock of his triumphs in the intellectual field. From that time onward his fall is rapid, and the first great crisis in his affairs arises when he finds out the sordid trap which has been laid by Arabella to bring about the marriage.

Much ink has been spilt over *Jude the Obscure*, and opinions vary to such an extent that it has been described by different critics as the worst [1] and the greatest [2] of Hardy's novels. He has been accused of making not a picture but a caricature of marital relations [1] ; and if the marriage of Jude and Arabella were intended to be representative there might be some truth in this accusation, but there is not the slightest shred of evidence that it is so meant. Jude himself is a man of exceptional ambition, perseverance and idealism, but he has one fatal flaw, and destiny and social ordinances cause the loss of all the benefit which might have accrued to mankind and to himself from these qualities—the first by throwing

[1] W. L. Phelps, *Essays on Modern Novelists.*
[2] H. C. Duffin, *Thomas Hardy.*

Arabella in his way, and the second by punishing a moral lapse by the imposition of a life sentence. The horrible pig-killing scene has a deep significance through the strong light it throws on the absolute incompatibility between husband and wife. The man who, as a boy, has rebelled against bird-scaring, from a feeling that the birds have a right to eat, is no fit mate for a woman who insists on a lingering death for the pig in order that the meat may bring an extra "shilling a score." A symbol may be traced, too, in the final scene of their quarrel: the smearing of Jude's beloved classics by Arabella's greasy fingers is symbolical of the smirching of his whole life by her low, stolid, soulless animalism. That marriages of this kind, in varying degrees, do occur, no observer will gainsay ; for reason is often completely blinded by emotion for a time, only to reassert itself too late, when an irrevocable step has been taken. And if there be dark shadows in the landscape, it is not the artist's business to paint the whole as though it were irradiated by sunlight.

Jude the Obscure contains two marriages which, though legal, are not real marriages in any true sense of the word—that of Sue, because she cannot respond emotionally to Phillotson, and that of Jude, because his soul is far above Arabella's comprehension. Yet current moral judgments would pronounce these .two alliances proper and virtuous and that between Jude and Sue immoral and vicious. There is no obvious remedy, but for the novelist this is beside

the point. His picture is a faithful one ; it represents
two people of high ideals, strongly attracted to each
other, possessing abundance of sympathy and many
common interests, unable tò throw in their lots together lawfully on account of " the letter " which
" killeth." Grant that both have erred grievously
and have brought punishment on themselves, that
punishment must surely be admitted to be excessive.
In the words of Hardy on the betrothal of Bathsheba
Everdene and Gabriel Oak may be found his clearest
statement of the *desiderata* for a successful marriage :

" Theirs was that substantial affection which
arises (if any arises at all) when the two who are
thrown together begin first by knowing the rougher
sides of each other's character, and not the best till
further on, the romance growing up in the inter-
stices of a mass of hard prosaic reality. This good-
fellowship—*camaraderie*—usually occurring through
similarity of pursuits, is unfortunately seldom superadded to love between the sexes, because men and
women associate, not in their labours, but in their
pleasures merely. Where, however, happy circumstance permits its development, the compounded
feeling proves itself to be the only love which is
as strong as death—that love which many waters
cannot quench, nor the floods drown, beside which
the passion usually called by the name is evanescent
as steam." [1]

Tess, Jude and Sue are by no means the only
victims of convention ; Elfride falls before it also,

[1] *Far from the Madding Crowd*, pp. 456-457.

and Giles Winterborne meets his death through a scruple. *For Conscience' Sake*, one of the short stories in *Life's Little Ironies*, turns on an interesting case of conscience arising out of an illicit union. The bachelor Millborne is dissatisfied with himself " as a specimen of the heap of flesh called humanity " because he has betrayed a woman twenty years before. His belated " reparation," however, is unwelcome to the woman ; he has to use all the arts of persuasion to obtain her consent to a marriage, and when the marriage is embarked upon it upsets the whole equanimity and life of both mother and daughter. His letter from abroad, after his departure from the scene of his error of judgment, begins :

" I have learnt that there are some derelictions of duty which cannot be blotted out by tardy accomplishment. Our evil actions do not remain isolated in the past, waiting only to be reversed : like locomotive plants they spread and re-root, till to destroy the original stem has no material effect in killing them."

From the point of view of strict convention Millborne has acted correctly : from the point of view of plain common sense he has done more harm than good ; and one of the reflections which must arise from a sympathetic perusal of Hardy's work is that an excessive regard for convention is always productive of this result.

CHAPTER VII

OCCUPATION

A MAN's tastes, manners and outlook on life are certainly conditioned to a certain extent by the calling he pursues day by day for his livelihood. The physician develops a "manner," the clergyman a particular tone of voice, and so forth : the members of different trades and professions often bear traits which can readily be recognised by an observer possessing the acuteness of a Sherlock Holmes, who, it will be remembered, could sum a man up fairly accurately from his gait, clothing and demeanour. At the same time, the novelist must guard against putting forward mere types instead of living, moving figures possessing well-marked idiosyncrasies over and above the general characteristics common to members of a class. Rymer, called by Macaulay "the worst critic who ever lived," urged the doctrine of conformity to type, saying that young men should always be represented as fond of sport and old men as querulous and avaricious, and the tendency to follow this reasoning is a frequent source of weakness in writers of fiction. Lawyers who were all rogues and squires who were all drunkards have

159

been succeeded by heroes who are always square-jawed, strong and silent, and heroines who are deep-eyed and intense. Having dealt with other prominent environmental influences and their relation to the working out of personality, it remains to consider the force exerted by occupation and to determine whether Hardy has gauged it accurately or whether he has, in any instance, kept too closely to type. The remaining characters (including some half-a-dozen figures of major importance and a number of less account) may be divided into five groups according to their occupation : (*a*) Agricultural and kindred workers ; (*b*) Soldiers and sailors ; (*c*) Men of business ; (*d*) The leisured ; (*e*) Professional men.

(a) *Agricultural and Kindred Workers*

Far from the Madding Crowd is the most complete picture of farm-life that Hardy has given us. Mr Beach [1] notes the " smack of irony " in the title, and it is indeed strange that this has not been more generally commented on unless critics have refrained from making the observation because of its obvious-. ness. The society with which the book deals is simple enough : the main interest centres in two farmers (a man and a woman), a shepherd, a sergeant of dragoons and a servant-maid. The scene is indeed " far from the madding crowd," but even here there is " ignoble strife " enough and to spare, in the shape

[1] In *The Technique of Thomas Hardy*, p. 61, 1922.

of overmastering passion, a betrayal, followed by the tragic death of the betrayed, blighted love, unhappy marriage and a murder! It is Mr Beach again who tells how the plot was provided from an outside source and sold also to Pinero,[1] and who lays his finger on the essential point in the novel when he says: " It is her [Bathsheba's] position of Weatherbury farmer that accounts for the appearance of such a character in English fiction." [2] For Bathsheba is none other than our familiar friend the " new woman," appearing five years before *A Doll's House* (1879). It is not through any startling challenge to established conventions that she earns this title : Sue Bridehead is the woman who throws down the gauntlet with most decision. But Sue comes at the end of a line which includes Ethelberta and Paula, and begins with Bathsheba—a group of women who, at first, definitely eschew dependence on men and set out to make their careers by their unaided exertions. Bathsheba's activities are directed towards farming by her inheritance. She early shows a decided and independent spirit in her relations with her workpeople ; her courage is evinced by her visits to the corn-market, a young, feminine figure in the crowd of experienced farmers ; her business-like and capable nature is made manifest by the determined way in which she faces the difficulties incident on her position. Two pictures of her early in the book display the different sides of her personality. Oak's

[1] *Op. cit.*, p. 6.   [2] *Op. cit.*, p. 58.

view of her, riding astride a pony and calmly performing an almost acrobatic feat in order to pass under
some low-hanging branches, gives a foretaste of the
severely practical Bathsheba. But his earlier view of
her, on the summit of a wagon-load of goods, un-
wrapping a mirror in order to look at her reflection,
reveals the intensely feminine, primitive Bathsheba,
who plays Hyde to the Jekyll of the other, and causes
so much heart-burning and trouble in later days.

The irrational, masterful and sometimes petulant
side comes out in her treatment of Oak. He is much
too blunt, plain and direct to make an immediate
conquest of her, and, to a nature like hers, his simple
loyalty merely invites the cavalier treatment which
it receives. She is glad enough to avail herself of
his knowledge and assistance when in trouble, but,
like many a man in such a case, he fails to make
progress on account of undue submissiveness, which
(as Hardy elsewhere shows) is not the way to the
feminine heart. Bathsheba, in spite of her gifts of
management and prudence in agricultural affairs, is
full of the " old Eve." It urges her to the freak of
sending the valentine to Boldwood (the one man in
the market who takes no notice of her) ; it makes
her careless of Oak's feelings ; and it brings her as
victim to the impudent Troy, whose wooing culmin-
ates in a statement that he has seen a more beautiful
woman and that his constancy cannot be counted on
unless the wedding takes place at once. Her thoughtless irruption on the placid life of Boldwood releases

forces more powerful than she can understand. She is washed out of her depth by the strength of his passion. The most hare-brained freak of all is her marriage with Troy, whose attraction, she well knows, is but an outward dazzle, and whose worthlessness she begins to find out at the very commencement of their life together. The courage, good sense and foresight developed in the practice of her business fail entirely to make their influence felt on her emotional side. She has to pass through shame, agony and tragedy before she reaches her haven of refuge, and when she does luckily reach it the shadows of a murdered husband and a would-be husband confined as a criminal lunatic remain to cloud her peace.

The male farmer in the same book, Boldwood, is materially successful, but the interest aroused in him has little or no relation to his occupation. First and foremost he is a deeply serious man, of set purpose and strong emotion. It is the innate constitution of his character that works out his destiny and ultimately wrecks him :

" That stillness, which struck casual observers more than anything else in his character and habit, and seemed so precisely like the rest of inanition, may have been the perfect balance of enormous antagonistic forces—positives and negatives in fine adjustment. His equilibrium disturbed, he was in extremity at once. If an emotion possessed him at all, it ruled him; a feeling not mastering him was entirely latent.

Stagnant or rapid, it was never slow. He was always hit mortally, or he was missed." [1]

Once the balance of his sentiments is disturbed, he becomes passion's slave, and a most abject slave, having lived to the age of forty without thinking of women, and so accumulating a reserve of emotion which is suddenly let loose. Boldwood is so straight-forward, sincere and whole-hearted that the feeling he inspires is one of admiration tempered with pity, and such a devotion as his is not to be lightly mocked at. Nevertheless it is undoubtedly true that he is entirely lacking in sense of humour, that he is prone to attach too much importance to small things, and that the headstrong and occasionally violent disposition he shows is indicative of a grave deficiency in balance and self-control, especially in view of his age and presumable knowledge of the world.

Gabriel Oak, on the contrary, possesses in eminent degree those virtues of restraint and self-mastery in which Boldwood is so conspicuously wanting. Though but a shepherd, he gives an impression of dignity and strength. He does this partly through the stoical resignation with which he submits to a very difficult position, and partly through the sheer efficiency which marks his performance of every task. Oak is the complete shepherd. In everything appertaining to the care of sheep, the nurture of lambs, the shearing and washing, he is a past master. His activities are not confined to this, however. He

[1] *Far from the Madding Crowd*, p. 137.

displays quick resource in dealing with the fire at Weatherbury, and it is he who foresees the storm and sets to work to thatch Bathsheba's ricks as a protection against foul weather. By this quality of skill and readiness he makes himself well-nigh indispensable to Bathsheba : it is he and he only who can perform the operation which is necessary to save the lives of her sheep. And even apart from professional matters, she comes to rely upon him for counsel in personal difficulties, respecting his opinion though its bluntness may (and does, several times) offend her. The generosity of Oak's affection is apparent when he carefully avoids disparaging his rival, Boldwood : his warning against Troy is quite disinterested ; he is so careful not to push attentions which he feels would be unwelcome after the tragedy that Bathsheba misconstrues his motives, attributing to contempt an attitude which really springs from delicacy. She discovers at last that she cannot do without him, and intermingled with affection and respect for his good qualities as a man is the feeling that in any emergency, in any difficulty connected with material things, she can depend upon him absolutely. He who was the complete shepherd has also become the complete farmer.

These three, of course, are only taken as examples of the agricultural worker. It is obvious that any full account of those whose work is more or less definitely connected with the land would take in more than half Hardy's characters, including many of those

165

dealt with under other headings in this book. The long line of peasants comprises milkmaids, field-labourers, woodcutters, shepherds, millers, carters and a dozen other callings, some account of which the second and third chapters of this study have attempted to give. One conspicuous fact will emerge from the consideration of Hardy's dealings with the different trades—namely, his admiration for thoroughness and efficiency. He dwells lovingly on Winterborne's skill in woodcraft, on Marty's proficiency in her humble capacity as maker of spar-gads and stripper of bark, on Crick's management of the dairy, on Oak's mastery of things ovine. One of the redeeming features of Fitzpiers (fully recognised by Grace even in her darkest moments) is his eminent capability in his profession. Such capability, apart from its intrinsic value, must always show a certain amount of industry and application. It may be noted in passing that Venn's livelihood is gained by an occupation (that of reddleman) which accentuates his solitary and mysterious aspect, making him a bogey to little boys.

(b) *Soldiers and Sailors*

Hardy's interest in history and genealogy has already been noticed, so that it is not surprising to find him bringing soldiers on his stage fairly frequently ; for an interest in the pageantry of soldiering usually goes hand in hand with a taste for the historic past. In *The Dynasts*, apart from the large-scale battle scenes, there are scenes introducing groups of privates, wherein the men are depicted as men first of all, thinking of home and sweethearts in Wessex rather than of military glory. Some of the poems also, on the Boer War and the European War, express a sense that to the participators in war it contains little romance. Nevertheless, Hardy's treatment of military figures is somewhat out of the line of his usual procedure in being predominantly romantic. The conjecture might be hazarded that, while he knows his rustics and farmers intimately, he is drawing less on personal experience and more on ballad and legend in respect of the hussars and dragoons. The result is a certain falling-off in power where these are concerned.

Sergeant Troy, in *Far from the Madding Crowd*, is the most notable study. The chapter heading, "Troy's Romanticism," shows that the conception of him as a figure of romance was quite clear and definite in the author's mind. He is, in most respects, a conventional figure. He is true to type in his more attractive qualities—smartness, ready wit, dexterity and a kind of swashbuckler elegance—and in his vices—impudence, drunkenness, selfishness, insincerity and callousness in love. *The Trumpet Major* is avowedly a romance, and is, in fact, a light and pleasant story : Anne's sufferings do not attain tragic pitch, and the pathos nowhere reaches the intensity of the greater novels. Amid the brightly

coloured camp scenes move the brothers Loveday
and the squire's son, Festus Derriman, in rivalry
for the hand of Anne. The time is out of joint;
war is the business of the hour. Festus is bold in
speech but cowardly in conduct, ridiculous in bombast
and bravado. From Ensign Northerton onwards,
his like has appeared many times in English fiction,
and is now a little wearisome. John Loveday is an
estimable character enough in himself; but he is
much too refined to be natural, much too capable
of appreciating fine shades of feeling, considering
his environment and especially the type of man with
whom he would associate. The qualities which gain
promotion for the ranker to the position of non-
commissioned officer are not usually those of gentle-
ness and consideration for the feelings of others.
The amenities of life are not learned in the barrack-
room, nor is the canteen a school of manners.

There are references in this book and in *The
Dynasts* to the York Hussars, a regiment of Hano-
verians employed in the British service at the time
of the Napoleonic wars. The idea of these men,
exiled from home, fighting in the cause of another
country than their own, seems to have touched
Hardy's imagination. The picturesqueness of their
uniforms, foreign moustachios and bearing impresses Wessex people, and some sympathy is aroused
by the peculiarly detached and isolated position they
occupy, forced to take part in a quarrel which does
not vitally interest them. The attachment of a senti-

168

mental, blue-eyed German, afflicted with *Heimweh*, to an English girl, forms the subject of a short story: *The Melancholy Hussar of the German Legion* [1] (a title, by the way, which is a masterpiece). If Troy conjures up *The Banks of Allan Water*, this young man calls to mind *A Warrior Bold*.

Most of Hardy's soldiers are sentimentalists. Luke Holway, in *The Grave by the Handpost* (*A Changed Man*, etc.), feels that it is his reproachful letter which has caused his father to commit suicide, so that the body is buried at the cross-roads, after the old custom, instead of in the churchyard. When Luke returns a second time from the wars, covered with glory, and cannot find the headstone he has ordered to be erected (since the villagers have not moved the body), his overpowering sentiment of disgrace and self-reproach causes him to take his own life likewise. Captain Maumbry [2] gives up the army for the Church, but though he is not a successful preacher he proves himself a hero. John Clark,[3] coming like Millborne to make belated reparation to his lady, is mortally stricken by the news of her betrothal to another. Captain de Stancy [4] delights to indulge sentimental regrets for his past misconduct by weakly giving in to Dare's whims and by exacting from himself a morbid avoidance of women's company.

The two sailors, Newson [5] and Bob Loveday,[6]

---

[1] *Life's Little Ironies.*   [2] *A Changed Man.*
[3] *Enter a Dragoon* (*A Changed Man*, etc.).   [4] *A Laodicean.*
[5] *The Mayor of Casterbridge.*   [6] *The Trumpet Major.*

are bluff, hearty and generous, as all good sailors are supposed to be. Bob adds, over and above these requirements, fickleness in love and the kind of simplicity which allows him to be easily imposed upon by such an adventuress as Matilda Johnson.

Hardy's soldiers and sailors, in short, are less convincing than any of the other personages in his novels, and bear but faintly the stamp of his individual genius.

(c) *Men of Business*

Since *The Mayor of Casterbridge* is the great town novel of the series, it is fitting that it should contain the two most prominent men of business that he has given us. Others there are, like Melbury, who take minor parts in a story, or who, like Ethelberta, display pronounced business ability ; but Henchard and Farfrae are the two most important men whose daily lives are mainly spent in buying and selling. Henchard is the most imposing male character that Hardy has ever drawn. His nature is a mixture of strength and weakness ; in him powerful opposite forces wage war. Sullen obstinacy strives with open heartiness, envious spite with good-nature, meanness with generosity, licence with restraint. The dogged determination of the man is superb. Drink has caused him to disgrace himself as a young man, so he takes a vow of abstinence and rigidly keeps it for the term of years ; he raises himself from the humble position of hay-trusser to that of a thriving corn-merchant and mayor of the town : when his sins come home to roost, and first Susan and then Lucetta appears on the scene, he does his best to repair former errors. But fate seems to deliver him one stunning blow after another, leaving him at last friendless, crushed and broken, to die untended and alone. In Wilde's *Picture of Dorian Gray* the young man per-forms what he considers to be a generous action, and draws aside the curtain to see whether it is registered on the features of the terrible picture ; but he finds that the only change in the hideous thing is the addition of a hypocritical leer to its lips. Henchard's intentions are good, but every attempt at atonement for past actions seems to be met by a similar leer from life. The very stars in their courses seem to work against him : even the weather seems to change wilfully in such a way as to do him harm. The child on whom he decides to lavish his care proves to be not his own but Newson's ; when he has made up his mind to marry Lucetta she no longer wants him as a husband ; the vagabond woman he has to try in his capacity of magistrate proves to be the crone who knows of the sale of Susan at Weydon-Priors. But the chief agency working to bring about Henchard's ruin is the uncompromising rigidity of his own personality, to which must be added the occasional outbursts of violence or intemperance. This inelasticity of character manifests itself in his

171

business dealings, wherein he holds fast to old-fashioned and haphazard methods, and tends to despise not only new mechanical aids but even such a *sine qua non* as accurate book-keeping.

Farfrae, on the contrary, "typifies the ingress of new methods and ideas into Wessex." [1] He brings exactitude of procedure into Henchard's yard, introduces a mechanical sower, and exercises extreme shrewdness in all his transactions. He is free and frank, kindly and sensible. It is through no callousness or ingratitude on his part that Henchard's position is made worse ; he never allows personal considerations to cloud business issues, but it is Henchard's own wrong-headedness and spite that pull him down. That Farfrae should succeed where the old Mayor fails—in love, commerce and social life—is but natural, though there are many factors which make his success very bitter to his rival. For Farfrae has the poise which brings success, whereas Henchard, though in many ways a grand and imposing figure, entirely lacks it, and through want of it compasses his downfall. Superstition is a strong element in his character, and it is this which precipitates his financial ruin. The business-man who should consult a "conjuror" as to the probable fluctuations of his market might thrive for a period, but his bankruptcy would be only a matter of time.

[1] S. C. Chew, *op. cit.*, p. 66.

(d) *The Leisured*

" County people " and persons of independent means do not generally figure to advantage in the Wessex Novels. Such circles as those described in *The Hand of Ethelberta* and *The Well-Beloved* suffer from one great defect—artificiality. Their cleverness is forced, their epigrams seem thought-out rather than spontaneous, their humour is laboured and their emotions are feeble beside those of creations like Boldwood, Winterborne, Tess, or even Elfride. Hardy might have been well advised to leave the *beau monde* to his contemporary and friend, George Meredith, for his own attempts to depict it are unconvincing and lack the sureness of his rustic scenes. Sincerity and genuineness of pure emotion are not the preserve of any section of the community : " Kind hearts are more than coronets," but even the possessor of a coronet may own a kind heart too. Bernard Shaw's John Tanner, in *Man and Superman*, when he points out how proudly his chauffeur speaks of his council-school, quite justly says that no Eton man could fling his place of upbringing in the world's face more arrogantly. The punctiliousness of butlers is almost proverbial ; the contempt of the skilled artisan for the unskilled is notorious.

Of D'Urberville and Mountclere enough has been said, for both are stock types of the " titled libertine " genus. Three women moving in county society, however, are more provocative of interest.

CHARACTER AND ENVIRONMENT

Miss Aldclyffe, patroness of Cytherea Graye, the heroine of *Desperate Remedies*, displays startling inconsistencies of temperament. Her moods succeed one another like phases of April weather. In spite of her proud and imperious temper, which at first drives Cytherea almost to despair, she is capable of softer feelings, and her sentimentalising over the orphan girl is at times even morbid. There is nevertheless some excuse for it, which is more than can be said for her excessive complaisance in respect of Manston, though here the tie is of course stronger. It comes as something of a shock to learn that this *grande dame* is the mother of Manston, but it explains much.

Felice Charmond exhibits some traits similar to those of Miss Aldclyffe (in her attitude towards Melbury and her weak confession to Grace, for instance), but on the whole she is less severe and unbending, perhaps because she is still young. She is like Fitzpiers in her delight in playing with an emotion, turning it over and gloating over it, and like him in her respect for family and position. She is a coquette of the more dangerous kind, who amuses herself by playing with fire, and is a *poseuse* withal, even to herself, for the occasion of her last quarrel with the physician shows the superficial nature of an affection which she takes quite seriously.

Viviette Constantine [1] is the most estimable of these ladies of leisure : indeed the only blots on her

[1] *Two on a Tower.*

174

character are the somewhat excessive regard she has for her social position, which moves her to keep the marriage secret, and her deceitful action in saving her reputation by wedding with the Bishop. Her love for Swithin is the more beautiful in having an almost maternal tincture in it. She takes a pride in his talents and work as well as in his good looks, and her self-sacrifice is great in sending him away in order that he shall not forfeit his annuity, though her whole heart is given to him, and she feels that absence and increasing years will damp his ardour.

(e) *Professional Men*

The three young architects, Springrove,[1] Smith [2] and Somerset [3] are all enthusiasts for their profession. No doubt a considerable amount of autobiographical material is embodied in their conversation, reflections and tastes in respect of architectural matters. As characters of fiction they present no outstanding features. All three are keen to make headway in their work, and all three do, in the end, attain large measure of success. The careers of Springrove and Smith show the social difficulties which beset the path of a professional man whose home is a lowly one. Springrove is disgusted that so much work is obtained by dining-out and influence rather than by merit, and Smith is forced to keep secret the

---

[1] *Desperate Remedies.*   [2] *A Pair of Blue Eyes.*
        [3] *A Laodicean.*

trade and place of residence of his father. Somerset's commission at Stancy Castle is given more on the strength of the personal interest which Paula takes in him than on account of his professional skill, about which Paula knows very little. Still, his conversation on architecture with the ignorant but pretentious Havill impresses on Paula that he knows his business, and when his plans are finished they are, in fact, found to be eminently suitable, not only making the place fit to live in, but also preserving its historic character.

St Cleeve, the astronomer,[1] is so absorbed by his celestial studies that for a long time he is unable to perceive the growing feeling for him that is arising in Viviette's bosom. When at last affairs reach a crisis he reveals a severely practical habit of mind engendered by the nature of his pursuits, and we feel that his love never rises to the same heights as Viviette's. Always (at least in his saner moments) he is as much devoted to astronomy as to Viviette. The anticipation, by an American, of his discovery is enough to reduce him to the blackest depths of misery, while the appearance of a new comet helps to cure him of an illness. He is never taken captive so completely by love as he is by science, which remains his true mistress to the end.

Phillotson,[2] like Jude, desires to enter the University and afterwards take orders. He starts a little farther up the ladder than Jude, but makes no more

---

[1] *Two on a Tower.*   [2] *Jude the Obscure.*

progress and remains a village schoolmaster. He is rather a pathetic figure of failure. His deficiencies, such as they are (and they are not serious), are those induced by a cramped, lonely, narrow and profitless life spent in drudgery, from which he is in no wise able to escape. That this weary, shabby, middle-aged man should conceive an infatuation for a complex, capricious, minx-like creature such as Sue Bridehead, is his misfortune : that she should marry him in a fit of pique at Jude's intemperance is a disaster to all three, but a disaster which cannot be laid at Phillotson's door. When the time comes for Sue's departure Phillotson behaves with the most chivalrous broad-mindedness, and Sue tells Jude that she was never so near loving the schoolmaster as when she left him. He is perhaps obtuse in not seeing that her return to him is only a freak of conscience, but again it is impossible to attach too much blame to his conduct. He has never come into the orbit of such personalities as Sue's, and is therefore incapable of comprehending her feelings and motives. But that is no fault in him, and in his generous renunciation he shows something like heroism, especially as it entails not only loneliness and loss of a bride, but also renewed penury and a large measure of social ignominy.

*　　*　　*　　*　　*

One of the marks of greatness in a literary artist is the power to unravel the tangle of conflicting motives and deal faithfully with many varieties of human character, weaving out of their multi-coloured strands a pattern full of beauty. When the artist can do this successfully no considerations of a personal nature, no leanings towards a particular class or creed ought to mar the critic's judgment or create a prejudice in his mind. It may be true that Thomas Hardy sees more of the dark side of life than of the bright side. But it cannot be said that he distorts character and event to fit in with a preconceived theory ; his theory is drawn from the facts as he observes them. And however much we may feel that in his works man is a helpless puppet in the grip of fate, however much our self-conceit may recoil from his conception of the comparative insignificance of humanity in the cosmic scheme, we must be sensible of the light he throws on many beautiful aspects of existence ; and the most beautiful of all is the spectacle of mankind undaunted, bearing trouble with fortitude, hating cruelty and injustice, and ever aspiring, albeit ineffectually, towards the heights.

WORKS CONSULTED

A

HARDY, T. *Works* (Wessex Edition), 20 vols. 1912.
— *Works* (Pocket Edition). Various dates.
— *A Changed Man*, etc. (Pocket Edition). 1919.
— *Satires of Circumstance.* 1914.
— *Moments of Vision.* 1917.
— *Late Lyrics and Earlier.* 1922.
— *The Famous Tragedy of the Queen of Cornwall at Tintagel in Lyonness.* 1923.

B.—*Works exclusively devoted to Hardy*

ABERCROMBIE, L. *Thomas Hardy : A Critical Study.* 1912.
BEACH, J. W. *The Technique of Thomas Hardy.* 1922.
CHEW, S. C. *Thomas Hardy, Poet and Novelist.* 1921.
CHILD, H. *Thomas Hardy* ("Writers of the Day"). 1916.
DUFFIN, H. C. *Thomas Hardy : A Study of the Wessex Novels* (2nd edition); with an Appendix on the *Poems* and *The Dynasts.* 1921.
JOHNSON, L. P. *The Art of Thomas Hardy.* 1894.

WORKS CONSULTED

MACDONNELL, A. *Thomas Hardy* (" Contemporary Writers "). 1894.

SAXELBY, F. O. *A Hardy Dictionary.* 1911.

SHERREN, W. *The Wessex of Romance.* 1908.

WEBB, A. P. *Bibliography of the Works of Thomas Hardy, 1865-1915.* 1916.

WHITFIELD, A. S. *Thomas Hardy : The Artist, the Man and the Disciple of Destiny.* 1921.

C.—*Works containing Chapters on Hardy, or extensive References to his Work*

CROSS, W. L. *The Development of the English Novel.* 1902.

CUNLIFFE, J. W. *English Literature during the last Half-Century.* 1908.

DAWSON, W. J. *Makers of English Fiction.* 1905.

FREEMAN, J. *The Moderns : Essays in Literary Criticism.* 1916.

HOWELLS, W. D. *Heroines of Fiction.* 1901.

MURRAY, D. C. *My Contemporaries in Fiction.* 1897.

PHELPS, W. L. *Essays on Modern Novelists.* 1910.

SCOTT-JAMES, R. A. *Modernism and Romance.* 1908.

SELBY, T. G. *Theology of Modern Fiction.* 1896.

SHARP, W. (" Fiona Macleod "). *Papers, Critical and Reminiscent.* n.d.

SYMONS, A. *Thomas Hardy* (in *The Encyclopædia Britannica*, 11th edition). 1911.

WALKER, H. *The Literature of the Victorian Era.* 1913.

WATSON, Sir W. *Excursions in Criticism.* 1893.

INDEX OF NAMES

*(The characters best known by their Christian names are
indexed thereunder)*

181

INDEX OF NAMES

182

INDEX OF NAMES

INDEX OF NAMES

184

INDEX OF NAMES

INDEX OF NAMES

186

INDEX OF NAMES

187

INDEX OF NAMES

188

INDEX OF NAMES